Praises For

Not in the FIRE

This is a book I could not put down when I started to read. After each chapter I keep asking, 'What is happening next to the characters involved?' As a pastor for over 50 years and dealing with many hurting families suffering from physical, verbal, and emotional abuse, the main character in this story is so typical of individuals and families we work with today in pastoral ministry. Author Barbara Austin shares how her faith in the Lord Jesus for daily sustaining help, healing and hope brought her to a better life. Believe me, once you start to read this book, you won't want to put it down.
—Pastor David Levandusky, Living Waters Assembly of God, Greenfield, MA., Author of the current third edition of the popular book titled, "The Last Eleven Days of Jesus. Countdown to Passover, Crucifixion and Resurrection. A scholarly resource showing the most accurate Four Gospel Harmony and Chronological order of Jesus Last Eleven Days."

***

In "Not In The Fire," Barbara Austin opens her heart and shares a devastating account of the unimaginable violence, abuse and injury she has witnessed and endured. But it's also the story of how God can redeem any situation, no matter how heartbreaking, through simple faith and obedience. "Not In The Fire" will be an encouragement for anyone looking for hope and a path to overcoming life's challenges.
—David Rhenow, weekday morning host at Life Changing Radio, WSDK, Hartford, CT; former missionary with Trans World Radio on the island of Guam.

***

Barbara Austin has been a friend for more than twenty-five years. Her life story reads like a Greek tragedy and a tale of suffering patience. I am familiar with the still small voice that speaks to her in her darkest most desperate moments. Her trust in Christ has seen her through events and experiences that would have broken the bravest hearts. I encourage you to read Barbara's story, to hear her share the struggles she endured and to listen for that voice yourself.

—Rev. Charles Tyree, pastor for 44 years (now in Norwich, CT), author "James: The Righteous Life That God Desires," and police chaplain

***

I met Barbara Harris when my late wife, Ida, and I began a ten-year pastoral ministry in Greenfield, MA in 2000. Barbara was faithful in bringing her girls to church and providing a stable, loving home environment. I learned some of her disastrous background then, but this book is a revelation. It reminds me of a Biblical promise to bring beauty out of ashes. I am amazed at God's grace and Barbara's tenacity to provide a home for all of these years. Ida and I enjoyed a closeness with the girls as if we were grandparents.

"Walk with Barbara through the pains and losses and gain hope."

—Reverend Art Warner, Retired Pastor who served over fifty years with the Christian and Missionary Alliance in church in Missouri, Iowa, Massachusetts and Maine as well as shorter teaching assignments in Kenya, New Zealand, Belarus and Alberta, Canada. He is the author of "Nuggets Gathered Along the Trail: 30 Principles to Help You Walk Victoriously With God."

***

I highly recommend "Not in the Fire" to everyone who has ever suffered emotional, physical, and psychological wounds. I was deeply moved to discover that our dear Sister experienced such terrible trials. She's an amazing woman and an incredible overcomer. This account demonstrates the unlimited power of God Our Loving Heavenly Father to do the impossible. He often spoke to Barbara through a "...still small voice", restored her fractured life by giving her a New Beginning in Christ. You too can have restoration and hope in a relationship with Jesus.

—Rev. Renzo Ventrice, Pastor & Evangelist, Redemption Gate Mission Society, Springfield, MA redemptiongate.org

***

Barbara's story is one of perseverance and trust in the Lord. This would be a good read for anyone who has experienced extreme difficulties in their life or who is currently experiencing struggles in life. Barbara's narrative is proof that God is good even when our circumstances are not.

—Rev. Jason Beamon, Lead Pastor, Greenfield Alliance Church, Master of Divinity, Crown College

***

Because of Barbara's faith in the Lord, she has that inner strength that helped her live through one of the hardest lives growing up. Women seek the comfort from good men and should be able to depend on strong, loving men that will help care for them and work with them as a team. Barbara came across men in her lifetime that let her down. With the whisper of God's word, Barbara was granted a life of blessings to give and share with others her hope and her strength!

—Jeffrey Baker, Financial Advisor, Family man and a man of God

Not in the

FIRE

Discovering God's will in a Gentle Silence

Barbara Austin

Published by KHARIS PUBLISHING, imprint of KHARIS MEDIA LLC.

Copyright © 2022 Barbara Austin

ISBN-13: 978-1-63746-141-9

ISBN-10: 1-63746-141-0

Library of Congress Control Number: 2022939858

All KHARIS PUBLISHING products are available at special quantity discounts for bulk purchase for sales promotions, premiums, fund-raising, and educational needs. For details, contact:

Kharis Media LLC
Tel: 1-479-599-8657
support@kharispublishing.com
www.kharispublishing.com

KHARIS
PUBLISHING

Author's Note

Some names and locations have been changed to protect the privacy of individuals. Memories are imperfect, but I've recalled the events related in these pages to the best of my knowledge.

Acknowledgments

I want to thank Wendy Black Farley, developmental editor for this project, for her tireless work to put my notes and tapes into words on paper and computer so I could work to update and move information around where it belonged as I added events initially forgotten. God bless her for her help to make this all come together!

I also want to thank Pastor David Levandusky for inspiring me to do this work, for reading the manuscript and instinctively adding all of the scripture verses where they fit into my life story. May God bless him for doing this when there are so many other things to do for the church and church family. It is very much appreciated!

And to my daughter Tonna Jean who has been behind me all these years. God bless and keep her! Amen

To Mary-Ruth for your spelling help and to Taylor and Rachel for your patience while I worked.

To my friend Nancy Snow who died before final completion. I appreciate her encouragement and her pushing me to do this book. I'll see you in heaven someday.

*"And after the earthquake a fire, but the **LORD** was not in the fire. And after the fire the sound of a low whisper."* I Kings 19: 12

"I had mentors to help me grow in the Lord, but I still clung to what I knew best- **-the still, small voice of God.** *I didn't want to lose that. I honestly thought people had noidea of my reality. So I prayed God would open their hearts to His voice as well. I didn't understand how anyone could survive by only reading [the Bible] and not the interaction with His voice. We need both!" – The Author (Page 102)*

Table of Contents

Prologue
Nestled Under the Nest

At first, I loved that three-story house on Grafton Street in Chester, VT. Therewas a big two-car garage and on the first floor were the kitchen, living room, and a big dining room. At the top of the stairs on the second floor was my mother's room. A right turn down the hall was my bedroom and across from me was my sister's room. There was also a small room next to them which was my brother's room. The bathroom was at the endof the hall. Just past my mother's room was a door to the third-floor attic where my Aunty Chicky stayed when she was visiting.

But this house is where the abuse started. I couldn't believe he would touch mein that way. The adults were having a party and had friends over. They were drinking, ofcourse. He came upstairs to use the bathroom. I knew his smell and his voice, so though it was dark, I knew it was him.

Chapter 1

Nestled in the Green Mountains

My life began before I was conceived. The Psalmist said God has knitted us together in our mother's womb, and He has a plan for us. The plan is not to harm us but to give us a future. (Psalm 139:13b; Jeremiah 29:11) I believe that with all my heart.

I felt loved as a small child, and I know my parents were in love with each other. There was a point in my early childhood when things changed, and the love imploded. I know why things fell apart, and I know who was responsible. That individual continued to make a mess of our lives in the same way during much of my life.

I'll start with my grandparents on both the Austin and the Grover sides. They often expressed confusion about why half their kids (older ones) had such terrible lives, though they raised them all the same. I think it's the lack of faith that played a part in why misery continued to infect their lives and many of the people around them.

My father's parents (Austin) were Episcopalian and went to the Lutheranchurch, St. Luke's, in Chester, VT. My mother's parents (Grover) were Advent Christian, and my fourth great-grandfather founded the Advent church in North Springfield, VT, where my mother's family attended when she was young. For some family members that is still the family church. I have alwaysloved that piece of my family's history. ("Train up a child in the way he should go; and even when he is old he will not depart from it." Proverbs 22:6)

However, I don't recall my parents practicing their faith. At times by choice, and at times for my safety, I spent time with my Grandparents Grover. I loved that they went to church. It was one of my favorite things to do--the prayer, the Bible reading, the songs, the choir, and watching my Aunt Chicky sing. I wanted to sing in the choir when I grew up, and I did for years. I continued with the Bible reading as well.

My dad had dropped out of school to help when my grandfather, Clarence Austin, broke his back while working on their chicken farm. It took months for his back to heal. They had other animals also, but it was mostly a chicken farm. Dad wasn't the smartest of the four kids, and it didn't seem that unusual for the times to just give up on school if a child was needed at home. He had stayed back in the first and third grades, so he was behind his age mates by quite a bit and only had advanced to the seventh grade.

Following the recovery of my grandfather from his injury, Dad entered the Navy and had returned from service by the time he started dating my mom. Kenny, his brother, and my mother's sister, Mary, had justgraduated from high school, and they invited my parents to join them at their prom because both of my parents had missed their own.

My mother, Florence, had graduated the year before and chose not to goto her prom. My dad missed his because of the service. Kenny and Mary were an item all through high school so Mom and Dad were already acquainted. Together, they all went to the prom in June of 1947. Needless to say, Dad and Mom hit it off at the prom, and they were married in July of 1948. ("ThoughI walk in the midst of trouble, you preserve my life!" Psalms 138:7)

On October 14, 1949, my brother, Lloyd William, Jr., was born. On March 15, 1950, he died. Mother said it was her fault. They documented his death as pneumonia. He was born with a defective trachea, and a prosthetic breathing tube was inserted to keep him alive. Doctors said it would be temporary until his trachea was completely developed.

This was at a time when doctors frequently made house calls or telephone calls to their patients, so Mom was informed in a telephone call that Lloyd would have healed by that time, so she could pull the tube. Lloyd suffocated in my mom's arms. Mother suffered a breakdown and spent weeks in the hospital. It's possible she never got over it.

On October 16, 1951, my second brother, Dwayne Maurice, was born and died at birth, also under-developed. My mother again went to the hospital with a breakdown, not as long, but she still needed care for a time.

Mom may have suspected that working and breathing in the chemicals at the Goodyear rubber factory had something to do with the deformities of her first two babies because she quit working there in the fall of 1952. She was pregnant with me by that time.

I was born November 28, 1952. My dad called me Barbie. My earliest recollections in my crib before I could even walk were of being loved and cherished. Dr. Jackson was my doctor and his records show I was growing faster than most; he also noted that I had a particularly good memory.

When first married, Mom and Dad lived in the "doll houses" at Westview in Springfield, VT. After I was born, they moved to Chester Depot (January of 1953) at the train station apartment my grandfather found for them. Grandfather operated the steam train. Not only did we live in a cute little apartment, but the whistle of the train was a constant reminder of my grandfather's presence and of the quaint town we lived in. So picturesque is Chester Depot that it was the site of the 2008 Hallmark Christmas movie, *Moonlight and Mistletoe*, starring Candace Cameron Bure and Tom Arnold.

As I got older, the hiss of the brakes and the train's whistle were often a signal that my grandfather was coming to get me. He would often stop, get out, chat with my parents, and take me with him. I remember the many days he gave me a ride to the other end of Chester by the covered bridge. I loved pulling the whistle on those trips. I had a little stool where I watched Grandpa shovel coal into the firebox of the steam train. This steam train was used in Saxtons River, VT. Last I knew, they were still giving rides on that same route I took so many years ago--with a newer train, of course. The one my grandfather drove is in a museum in Steam Town USA.

My grandmother would meet us at the train, which had slowed considerably because of the crossroads, gather me in her arms, and take me to the farm for the day while my parents worked. Mom had taken a position with National Survey designing maps. Her designs for mapping the mountains were award-winning. She was always proud of that. My father worked as a bus driver and a janitor at a local high school through all of their marriage. He would pick me up in the evenings and take me home. It was a great life for about five years; the memories are vivid and wonderful. ("And we know that for those who love God all things work together for good." Romans 8:28)

[**Author's Note:** *As I reflect on this time of my life I can only think of how good it was--as it should have been. But as adults made bad decisions, those decisions impacted the lives of children who had no alternative but to be a part of such choices. The same is true for the good judgments. I and my choices have been no exception. This is a hard lesson.*]

Not in the fire

Chapter 2

The Winds of Change

It was the spring of 1955 when my life changed. My mom told my father that her boss raped her. It was devastating in so many ways. I found this out later on. She became pregnant as a result. ("Consider your ways." Haggai 1:7a)

My dad remained loving to my mother throughout the pregnancy and vowed he was going to take care of the baby as his own. There are notes in my baby book saying that as I played with toys on the bed with Dad and Mom I would put my head on Mom's belly and say, "tista." I cherish this image of us as a happy family.

Dad got a restraining order against mom's boss, Kenneth H., to stay away from her and the family, but no one moved to press charges. I wish they had. Perhaps then he wouldn't have bothered us all for what seemed like most of our lives. But it was all kept secret so that no one would know the difference.

Marie was born on January 7, 1956. In the aftermath of Marie's birth, at least for a time, things were okay. Dad took care of her and claimed her as his own. Jackie Haskal was a good friend of Mom's who watched us when they both worked. We had fun.

Dad took me fishing and we spent a lot of time together because I was older and remarkably close to my dad. He also displayed many signs of love for Marie. Despite all of the signs, I sensed something was different and picked up bits and pieces of conversations. I learned a lot by simply listening.

Later in life, I found out why and what had happened to Mom. Families talk, but it never seemed to get outside the extended family.

It was sad that Grandpa and Grandma Austin wanted nothing to do with Marie. They knew that she wasn't their grandchild. Marie never got to visit the farm or get to know them. It hurt her, I'm sure. Even though my dad acted as though everything was fine, I now realize the impact of Mom conceiving, bearing and rearing a child Dad knew wasn't his. ("Blessed is the person who finds wisdom, the one who gains understanding." Proverbs 3:13)

Eventually Dad showed other signs of how it undermined their relationship. He met somebody named Sally at the school where he worked. She was married, but soon after Dad and Sally started a relationship, she discovered she was pregnant with her husband's son, Tommy. Dad and Sally stopped talking and she remained with her husband. All this time, Dad was still living with Mom, who announced she was pregnant with another child.

Things started to get better again. My brother Brian was born in 1957 and my dad was so pleased to have a son. We seemed happy again.

Kenneth H. left National Survey and went back to Saxtons River where his wife and two children were living. His wife, June, suffered from severe depression and needed institutional care for much of the time her children were young. In those days, we were told such a placement was an "insane asylum."

I was six years old and Brian was one year old when Kenneth H. decided he wanted to visit Marie. Dad asked, "What do you think you're doing here? You know I'll call the police. You're violating the court order to leave us alone. So leave now and don't come back!" This was so upsetting to Marie, who thought my dad was also her dad. It rattled whatever normality we had achieved.

A few weeks later, Kenneth H. showed up again when Dad was working. My mom tried to slam the door on him but he was drunk and he forced his way in. I hid from him, but I could tell he was pushing my mom around. He said, "Marie is my daughter, and you have to let me see her. You know she is mine." Mom yelled back, "It doesn't matter. Lloyd is raising her as his. We're trying to get on with our lives." ("Hide me in the shadow of your wings." Psalms 17:8b)

My dad happened to come home from work while Kenneth H. was there. I don't know if he forgot his lunch or why he returned, but he walked in the door and saw Kenneth H. Predictably, they got into a shoving match followed by a big fight.

Kenneth shouted, "I'm here to see my daughter and son." Then he mocked, "Do you really think this is your son and that you're even man enough to have a son?" This horrible statement came back on him. God never allowed him to ever have another son, yet God gave my dad two more sons.

I'll never forget the look on my dad's face. My mother was hollering, "He's a liar! Lloyd. Look at him! He's your son, Lloyd. I have not cheated with this drunk. I don't want him around. Just make him leave."

My dad, for whatever reason, looked at Kenneth and looked at her and said, "I'm done. I can't do this any longer, Florence," and he walked out. It was so sad.

My mother bawled her head off. She shoved Kenneth out the door yelling, "I'm never going to get together with you! Just leave us alone. You know this is Lloyd's son." I watched the whole mess from my bedroom door and cried. I was scared and unsure what was going to happen to us and my mom. ("Who have eyes to see but see not, and ears to hear, but hear not." Ezekiel 12:2a)

[Author's Note: *As I look back at this time in my life, I see that this is where I started to become the strong one, the protector. I watched and listened to everything. I played with my toys while intently listening without anyone knowing. Adults would say, "She's ok. She's so into her toys." Or "She's just a little girl, she doesn't understand." I understood so much more than anyone imagined. My grandmother told me to always talk to God, and He would be there with me. She would never lie to me so I believed wholeheartedly! His voice was real and always has been!*]

"In the morning, O Lord you hear my voice; in the morning I lay my requests before you and wait in expectation." Psalm 5:3 (NIV)

Chapter 3

Fractured

Sally had gone back with her husband and she had Tommy around the same time Brian was born. Dad told Sally that Mom had another child by Kenneth. For some reason, dad wanted to believe it wasn't true.

That was when life again became a nightmare for me. My dad was gone and I had idolized my father. I was Daddy's little girl. He made me feel loved, and I missed him so much. ("Do not covet another man's wife!" Exodus 20:17)

By 1960, my dad had divorced my mom and married Sally, who had also divorced her husband. After the separation from Mom, Dad had lived on the farm with his parents. Sally lived with my dad's sister, Martha, until her divorce. My grandparents never got over the divorce. They were not fond of Sally at first. They liked my mother and were sick about the whole thing.

Based on my dad's say-so, eventually they believed my mom had been cheating. I was sad and have never been convinced my mom had done anything to deserve people doubting her. I still believe if she had just reported Kenneth to the police, and he had been arrested, prosecuted and put into jail, our lives would have been so much different; my family could have stayed intact.

Sally's husband was also a drunk and an abuser, just like Kenneth. I suspect her marriage would have ended, regardless of my parents' divorce.

Sally was pregnant with Michael Lloyd when she and Dad got married. Mom was furious because the name of her firstborn was used for Michael's middle name. Dad was fixated on having a son with his name.

During this time, Mom had trouble making ends meet financially, and Kenneth had kept up his endless attempts to be involved in her life. He seemed obsessed with her, perhaps because she was a beautiful woman. I loved to watch a show about a girl detective and I learned a lot from her, such as putting a glass against a door or wall to hear through it. That was how I found out a lot about what was going on and what was planned.

It was at this low point Kenneth exploited Mom's needs and played on her sympathy at the same time. It appeared his wife was indefinitely hospitalized and wasn't returning home. He was sober and said he was sorry for the way he behaved when drunk. He offered to support Marie, Brian, and me, too.

In exchange, he wanted Mom to take care of Keith and Susan, his two kids, for him. He said he would pay the rent on a three-story building on Grafton Street in Chester and we could live there. He explained that part of the deal was that Mom would not have to work, just stay home and raise the kids. He would also live in the garage apartment. Mom said she would think about it, but as time went on and bills piled up, it was clear to her that she could only find a part time job. She could not make it alone. She called Kenneth to talk.

I think it was at this point my grandfather told me a story that went like this: One day a farmer saw a snake in his garden and he raised his rake to kill it. It was frozen and half-dead. The snake begged him not to kill him, so the farmer took sympathy on the snake, picked it up and put it in his pants pocket. After a few hours, the snake, now warm, awoke and bit the farmer. The farmer removed the snake from his pocket and said, "Why? I trusted you." The snake just said, "Don't blame me. You knew I was a snake when you picked me up!"

My mom made it clear she would never marry Kenneth. This was an arrangement of convenience because she didn't want to lose her kids and didn't have a way of making enough money. She thought it was fair to let him pay her way because it was his fault Dad left her. It was his responsibility to support us all, thus she agreed. My dad had to pay child support for all three of us because we all had his name on our birth certificates, but it was not much and definitely not enough to survive on. Dad suggested many times he would take me but Mom refused. She wanted her kids to stay together.

Notes from this time indicate that I was very thin and pale. I liked to sing, dance, and play with my imaginary friend and Pug, my dog. My eyes turned from blue to green and I became nearsighted. Also, when Mom corrected me, I threatened to tell Dad. I bit Kenneth and kicked him when he visited. Visits were part of the agreement during the daytime only.

I also got what was recorded as the German measles and the Asian flu. I was extremely sick and was sent to Grandmother Grover for a time. At Gram's, I not only recovered, but I liked going outside again. When I returned home, we were settled into the big three-story house. Kenneth stayed in his apartment. ("And the one who trusts in Him will not be put to shame." I Peter 2:6 (NIV))

[**Author's note:** *This is one of the times in my life when so much is happening. I am only sharing the things God has put on my heart to share, though I can remember many events as though they were yesterday! I have a very sharp memory --a gift from God. Though young, I was seldom free to act like a child. I needed to be mature and grown up. So I was. I believe my childhood was taken from me. Sadly, kids understand more of the happenings in the adult world than one would expect. I saw and heard more than anyone was willing to admit. All through my life I kept secrets because I knew how easily I discovered the secrets of others. I made sure no one was listening through a wall or door to my room because I was guilty of doing this very thing with others.*]

"Lead me oh Lord, in your righteousness because of my enemies; make your way straight before me." Psalm5:8

"Let the little children come to me." Matthew 19:14

Not in the fire

Chapter 4

The Family Grows

Before my mom stepped in, she assumed Kenneth's kids, Keith and Susan, had a babysitter. ,When we went to get them to live with us, it appeared no one was in any way attentive to them. I remember as we approached the apartment on the second floor, a woman from across the hall opened her door and said, "About time. Those kids have been screaming for two days."

My mom said, "I'm sorry. That won't be a problem any longer. We are taking them with us." The lady slammed the door. ("Beloved, if God so loved us, we also ought to love one another." 1 John 4:11)

I'll never forget the scene as we walked into the apartment. Though he was six years old, Keith was in a crib and covered with feces. Bottles of sour milk were helter-skelter in his bed. The room reeked of urine. He was covered in urine burns. It was awful! I'd never seen anything like it. I remember turning away and saying, "Yuck!"

***

Mom sent me into the living room to meet Susan, who was eight years old. On my way, I observed dirty diapers. On the rare occasion the diapers had been changed, the soiled ones were just thrown on the floor. They were scattered all over the room and I stepped over them. It was so bad. All of this, even though Keith should have been trained and weaned years before.

Supposedly, Kenneth H. had told Susan to change Keith's diapers occasionally while he was gone and feed him a bottle. It was apparent she didn't know how to do any of that and the milk he left was sour since she had left it on a shelf. She was sitting in the living room on the couch, watching cartoons and eating anything she could get her hands on. There were boxes of stale cereal and crackers strewn about. She was dirty and needed a bath.

My mother mumbled, "This is how you take care of your children?" She gave them both a bath and clean clothes. Their father seemed embarrassed, for the moment. She looked at him and said, "You're cleaning up the mess!" He was gone for a week, and I supposed he was cleaning up the apartment.

There were now two more members in our family. Susan was one year older than I, and on the ride home I made it clear to her, whether she cared or not, if she was going to join our family, I was still the oldest. That's all there was to it. I didn't care when her birthday was. And she made it clear to me she didn't care if I took over the role of being the oldest because she didn't want to boss or care for anybody. She was very shy and kept to herself. She remained that way most of her life until she died years later--like her father--of alcohol consumption!

At first, I loved that three-story house, but that's where my abuse began. When things should have become easier, the house I loved became a place of uncertainty and stress. I was constantly on guard, as if it all was my responsibility. ("For each should carry his own load." Galatians 6:5 (NIV))

I started school in September of 1959. It was the first grade; I was older than the rest because I turned 7 in November the previous year. I hated school. I spelled my name Bboaarr. I walked to school. I did not like my teacher; she wouldn't let me go to the bathroom during class so I wet my pants and the other kids laughed at me. I was absent twenty-one days. I was afraid to leave my mother alone. I couldn't pay attention. I wasn't doing well!

I had a hard time with everything that year. My mom became room mother at my school and helped me be a snowflake in a play for Christmas. She also had to cut my hair short because the class got head lice. I hated it.

I was happy to go to Dad's for a week in the summer, and Dad taught me how to swim.

When I got home, we all went to "Uncle" George's camp at Lake Amherst for ten days. There we met Kenneth's family--new "aunts and uncles." I never felt close to any of them. I spent a lot of time alone swimming. After that I went to Bible camp with Gram Grover for two weeks and then I went back to Dad's until school started.

I entered my second year in first grade and I remember that the teachers, Margaret and Mrs. Macy, took us to Lake Spofford on a field trip. I walked to school with Virginia Kingsbury and Danny Williams. I had a

Not in the fire

crush on Danny but I never told him. In November I started going to Sunday School with my teacher, Mrs. Kinsley, at a Baptist church in Chester, VT. I didn't talk about Dad much at home, but I was happy to see him and very moody whenever he left. When he couldn't visit and only called, I cried until I was sick over not seeing him.

I was in the Christmas play again with only a singing part, got German measles again, and was sick for eleven days. Every one of us got them. It was not a lot of fun. There were lots of baking soda baths. A plus was Kenneth H. stayed as far away as he could since he had never had them as a child.

And I got my first pair of glasses, for which I was made fun of and called "four-eyes." To exercise my eyes, I was told to sit on the side of the road and write down all the license plate numbers for exercise. One day, Mom heard cars beeping and came running out of the house only to find I had moved my chair to the middle of the road. She grabbed me and said, "What on earth are you doing?" I told her I couldn't see the plates on the side of the road but I could in the middle. That was the end of that! There was no more license plate watching. I laugh now, but still feel, *how stupid could I have been?* ("Though I walk in the midst of trouble, you preserve my life." Psalm 138:7)

Kenneth H. didn't live in the house with us, as I said; that was part of the arrangement. He made a garage apartment. He was a ham radio operator and fixed TVs on the side during evenings after his day job back at the paper company. He also liked to fly a plane. He had learned to fly in the Air Force.

Each day he was allowed to come into the house during the day for a few hours to spend time with Marie. Strange as it was, he never asked to see Susan or Keith, only Marie. I started to slap Marie for no reason and wouldn't let any one touch Brian. He was my baby, and I did not like to share him. I was mean to Marie because she was accepting of Kenneth H. I saw her as a traitor to Dad.

Brian and I attempted to stay away from Kenneth H. and did our own thing. He was a drunk, on and off the bottle, over and over. When he was sober, he seemed okay. He wasn't as violent to my mother, but the times when he wasn't drinking were few. Mom had a car accident and Brian hit his head on the dashboard, followed by seizures. He outgrew those when he was around sixteen, but this made Mom very protective of her only son.

To explain when the abuse began, I have to go back to a weekend during that horrible first year of school. Kenneth H., my mother, and some friends had a New Year's party. The party goers had left really late, and

Kenneth H. came upstairs to use the bathroom, which was near my bedroom at end of the hall between the kids' bedroom and mine. ("Avoid every kind of evil." 1 Thessalonians 5:22 (NIV))

He came into my room and he molested me. I froze in fear as he touched me and thought, *what is he doing and why is he touching me like that?* I was so scared. I didn't know what to do. I knew it was him. I could smell him and hear him moan and utter some words. I didn't want to see what was going on and kept my eyes closed, as if to block out the horror.

When he left, I got up and went to the bathroom. I was trembling. I took a hot bath. I was determined never to let him touch me again. My anger for him turned to hatred! I kept running away from school to be home with my mother out of a sense of responsibility for what he might do to her or anyone else. As the oldest, I felt it was up to me to watch over them. I just could not trust him with any of them.

One evening when I thought everyone was asleep, I heard my mother scream. I ran down the hall, opened the door to Mom's bedroom, and saw him on top of her, naked. Her clothes were strewn all over the room along with his. As she struggled to get him off her, they looked up and saw me standing at the door. He swore at me, "Get the ---- out of here!" My mother cried out, "Just get out of here, Barbie. Go back to bed. I'll be okay."

I left. It got really quiet; there was no more noise. My mother never brought up that night or said anything about it. I think she prayed I would forget about it, but it doesn't happen that way. I think things could have been different if she had talked to me afterwards. It's what a parent should do. I wouldn't have thought wrong things myself that were not correct, specifically that she could not even take care of herself and protect herself from him. *So how on earth could she protect us?* In my mind, that meant it was up to me. ("God, in you do I take refuge." Psalm 7:1)

When school was about to end for the summer, my mother took me out two weeks early for what reason I never knew. She sent me to Dad for the summer vacation to stay with him and Sally.

Brenda, Sally's daughter, and her son Tommy and I got along well. We played and had fun. They lived in a tiny house that was surrounded by sumac trees. We played in the sumac trees, and Brenda wanted to make a soup with some of the berries the bushes produced. After handling the leaves and berries, Brenda became extremely sick. It was poison sumac, of course. She seemed deathly sick, and Sally took her to the doctor.

I remember her face was swollen and bright red. She was ordered to bed rest and Sally had to follow a strict regimen of bathing and medication to soothe the sores. Sally was especially stressed since she was pregnant with Patty and hoping she wouldn't get poison sumac herself. She didn't, but the upshot of her anxiety was that she told Dad I had to go home. She told him she had enough to deal with at the time.

I was sent back to Mom's house, but somehow ended up with my Grandparents Grover. It was September of 1960. It was about that time when Dad's divorce from Mom was final, and he married Sally. Soon after I left, and just before Patty was born, they all moved to a bigger place in Brattleboro, VT. The firehouse was at the bottom of the hill from them and my dad became a part-time fireman.

Summer was well over, and by the time I returned home I was twenty-four days late in joining second grade. As written on my report card, my second-grade teacher was Mrs. Latencies in Chester, VT, and my mom was signing my report card as Florence H. It was meant to make us look like a family, but they were not married. She still had my father's name.

I was angry again because of Kenneth H. and what he might do to Mom. She seemed to try to keep him out of our house and in his apartment. Even though she locked the door, there still were times he came in to see "his" kids. I always felt uncomfortable when he was there. But I never feared. ("There is no want to those who fear Him." Psalm 34:9 [New King James Version—NKJV))

Whenever he was around in the evening I would go where I was told to go by that "still, small voice." Gram Grover had told me the story about how Samuel in the Bible used to be called at night by God. She told me to just answer the way Samuel had, "Yes Lord," and He would tell me what to do like He did Samuel. So I did! I had no reason to not believe it wouldn't work for me too. ("For everyone who asks receives." Matthew 7:8)

That's when I had started hiding under beds, mine, my sister's, or my brother's. I would squeeze under the claw tub or hide in closets, wherever that "still, small voice" told me to go. Kenneth H. looked, but he couldn't figure out where I was. I had been doing this since that day he touched me.

My life was not all bad, however; I tried to make sure it was fun, too. Though we had very few friends come to our house, I played games with the kids, and I had a little bake oven my grandmother got me and cooked up cakes and cookies for them. The kids loved it. We had tea parties, played board games, made tents, and pretended to be pirates. We spent a lot of time just frolicking in the backyard and in winters we would make snow castles and slide all day. Brian had just one friend who played with us at the time. Brian Waldo was what we referred to as a midget. We later learned that was not how we should refer to our friend Brian. I'd never seen a small person before, but he was a cool kid and he played well with Brian. It was good for both of them.

I was aware that Mom was pregnant again soon after I had returned from a weekend visit to Gram's house, and the pregnancy was very obvious by April of 1961. I also had heard my Gram say to my Aunt Chicky, "Kenneth H. raped Florence again." I was stunned that Gram knew about what had happened to Mom before. I was always listening, even when I pretended not to be. I had to know what was going on, so I was almost always on my guard; it helped to pretend I was a detective.

One day I heard a scream that sounded like it was coming from the kitchen. I knew it was Mom. I hurried to the kitchen where Kenneth H. was shoving her against the sink. She was struggling with him; he was mean even though she was pregnant, and of course he was drunk. She had been washing dishes, and in the struggle she had dropped a fork on the floor.

I didn't want him to hurt her or the baby. I was a very bold child and I remembered the story about David and Goliath and David's bravery. He just trusted in God. I picked up the fork from the floor, prayed, and flung it at Kenneth H. Like David with Goliath, I was going to stop my giant. I let it go and it landed right in the middle of his forehead, just like David's stone landed on Goliath's forehead. I knew God helped me just as He helped David, for he was a bold child also. I loved my Bible stories and believed them. My favorites were the warriors, but I also loved Mary, sister of Lazarus, because she washed Jesus's feet with her hair; other people from the Bible flooded through my mind.

The wound drew blood, a lot of blood, in fact. He fell back and hit his head hard on the floor. My mother was panting in panic and sat me in a chair in the corner. She said, "Stay right there." She ran to Kenneth H. and saw that he wasn't dead. She pulled the fork out and wrapped his head in a towel. She called her mother, my grandmother Grover, and told her what I had done. She told her she must get me out of there. If she didn't, Mom said she was afraid that when he woke up, he would kill me.

My mother called some of his friends who carried Kenneth to his bed over the garage. They stayed and watched him till he woke up and was sober. He got a stern talking to by his friends and was told to leave us alone or he could get arrested for abusing a pregnant woman.

My grandmother arrived and I was packed and ready to go. In fact, I was eager to go. She lived in Springfield, VT, about twenty minutes away. They were genuinely concerned that I had to resort to violence to protect myself and others. Needless to say, they didn't like Kenneth H. at all. I was happy to be with my grandparents. Every day they drove me to school until school got out.

I remember the summer of 1961 as the one that changed my life. I was afraid to leave Mom, Brian and the kids alone, but Mom reassured me Kenneth H. would not be coming back into the house; she was sending him away as her father suggested, "Before he kills one of us." She did not want the state involved in our life, or my dad to take me from her, so everything was kept between us and my grandparents. ("I will instruct you and teach you in the ways you should go, I will counsel you with my loving eye on you!" Psalm 32:8 (NIV); "He trains my hands for battle." Psalm 18:34 (NIV))

[Author's Note: *As I reflect on this time in my life, this incident, besides displaying that I had become stronger and bolder, is also when I admitted to myself some of the facts about my family that I didn't like. I had to grow up fast, develop my own sense of how life should be, and I trusted very few people in my life. I wanted to depend on God, yet I did not understand what that truly meant. I did my best. I still depended on His voice to help me through each day.*]

Chapter 5

A New Beginning in Christ

During that summer at Gram's, among the many activities they provided, I went to Camp Bethel. I will never forget that experience. It was an awesome camp. We had gone there a number of times with my mother and my dad over my younger years, but I hadn't been there in quite some time.

I went with Ronnie, my cousin, and his wife-to-be, Ellie. They did so much for me. Ronnie lived with my grandparents and was always kind and special to me. He often babysat for me when Gram had to be away and we came to be known as the "kissing cousins" because we were so close. We loved each other like brother and sister. Though he was a lot older than me, in my childish foolishness I was convinced that I would marry him when I grew up. They also thought if I went with them, I'd open up more to Ellie, and I did.

I was tickled to death to accompany them to camp and my grandparents joined us later. I loved that time at the camp meeting. The pastor spoke about forgiveness and becoming clean, starting fresh, having the Lord in your heart and in your life. He told us to stand and pray if we wanted to follow Jesus. They sang the hymn, **Just As I Am**. I raised my hand, stood up, and said my prayer of salvation with him. I remember thinking, as once again the old guy kept saying, "Amen," *Will you be quiet? I haven't finished my prayer yet.* "I get it now, but kids are so literal. ("If anyone is in Christ, he is a new creation. The old has passed away: behold the new has come." 2 Corinthians 5:17, 18) I went home with a stronger understanding of the "still, small voice" that has never left me since I was a child. That "still, small voice" helped me again and again. In fact, He got me through the rest of my life and

Not in the fire

all I have been through.

In mid-August when I returned home, Kenneth H. was not gone. To make matters worse, I found out that he had been molesting Susan all of her life. That is when she and I became friends. I felt so badly for her and I talked about Jesus all the time. My "still, small voice" that evening woke me up in the middle of the night and told me to take my pillow, my blanket, and my stuffed animal and climb underneath the claw tub in the bathroom. So I did and stayed there and stared at the wall until I fell back asleep. I was safe there. I felt incredibly at peace under the tub. I paid no attention when someone came in to use the facilities! ("And I will give you a new heart, and a new spirit I will put within you." Ezekiel 36:26a)

Sometimes the voice told me to hide in the back of my closet. I made a tent with boxes in front of me. I would lie down and just enjoy the seclusion of that closet. I slept in there for the longest time. In the morning, no one knew where I was! I was always the last to use the bathroom and make my appearance downstairs. It was a good hiding place until Mom cleaned out the closet and dismantled my place to hide, and I was not happy about that.

In September of 1961 I was going into third grade with Mrs. Gray. I still did not like school. I was made fun of because I was behind, I wore glasses, and I was so skinny they called me "toothpick." One day at recess I was hanging upside down from the top bar of the jungle gym and someone thought it cute to push my legs so that I lost my grip and fell to the ground on my head. I was knocked out cold. Mom was called and she took me to the doctor's office be checked out. I stayed home for four days with a concussion, but they said I would be okay. No one was allowed to hang on the top bar of the jungle gym any longer and the wise guys couldn't get on it at all. I never went on it again. Instead, I spent the recess time on the swings until it was time to go back in to school. The evening, the "still, small voice" told me to go into the attic on the third floor. It was a place of comfort because it brought back memories of my Aunt Chicky staying with us; her guestroom was in the attic. She often let me bunk with her up there. I loved her so much!

There was a little trap door in the attic that led to another storage area. It was cold and damp and there were mice in there, but that was closed off and the side of the attic where I stayed was nice. There was a bed, bureau, desk, table and chair. There were finished walls and two windows. I could even lock the door leading up to what was for me, my safe room. ("Do not be misled: 'Bad company ruins good character'." 1 Corinthians 15:33 (NIV))

I got into the bed, looked above me and noticed a large paper wasp nest. I don't know how long it had been there, but it was a big one. I remembered Grandma Austin's paper wasp nest and how she said they would not hurt me. She had a big nest over her rocker on her porch for years. We used to sit and watch them. Thus, the "still, small voice" told me not to worry, just stay in bed and go to sleep. They were there to protect me. So I turned off the light and went to sleep. I liked the dark. I could see what was coming at me, but no one could see me. I never liked nightlights; one can hide better in the dark. God is my protection and my light!

I slept there many nights unnoticed, but eventually Kenneth H. found out. Whether it was the noise of the bed springs, I don't know. As he came up the stairs, I clung to the blankets. He laughed when he had pried open the door. "Well, finally found you!"

Just then, he looked up over the bed with his flashlight with panic on his face; he was allergic to the paper wasps. I watched as those wasps swarmed down and attacked him. He was stung repeatedly and was screaming as he went down the stairs. They retreated back to their nest as he slammed the door. He screamed in pain and shouted at my mother, "She is sleeping under a gigantic paper wasp nest."

Mom called the hospital and an ambulance came to get him. Then she came up part-way to see me and the paper wasp nest. She saw that they weren't bothering me. I told her, "I'm fine. I've been sleeping up here with them for a long time. The Lord is taking care of me."

My mother said, "Okay." She left me there. I didn't tell her why I had to hide, and she didn't ask. She also knew the wasps wouldn't hurt me if I wasn't afraid of them, and she wasn't afraid of them either. She also remembered Gram Austin's nest. And she knew I did not like Kenneth H.

He returned from the hospital a week or so later. (I so wished he had died.) I came home from school to discover he had taken a blow torch and killed the whole nest. In the process, he burned the ceiling; there were dead wasps and debris all over the bed. He bellowed, "Well, you won't be staying up there no more." I cried. Those wasps never hurt me and didn't deserve to die like that. I swept them all up and had a funeral for them in our back yard. I asked Jesus, "What do I do now?" ("I will fear no evil, for you are with me; your rod and your staff they comfort me." Psalm 23:4b)

Kenneth H. didn't bother me that night. The following day, I asked my mother if I could start spending the nights at a friend's house. I had made friends with Virginia Kingsbury during the second grade. Her parents were always kind to me. Though quite poor, they always seemed to have a garden and plenty of food. They welcomed me to spend the night often. They said I was too skinny and they needed to fatten me up. I loved it there. They knew I was very unhappy at home. I didn't want to be home, and Mom knew it. She never asked why.

Kendra was born on Nov 25, 1961, three days before my birthday. School records indicate I was prone to worry and stayed home a lot. I still didn't like school. But I loved to watch Kendra. She was like an early birthday gift, so happy all the time. I felt sad that Kenneth was her dad and she had to be named after him I wasn't mean to Marie any longer. I tried to take care of them all.

Christmas wasn't a big deal for us since we didn't get much for presents. Soon after Christmas the year Kendra was born, Kenneth H. moved to Saxtons River with his parents, taking Keith and Susan with him. I had grown closer to both of his kids and felt so sorry they had to go with him.

A few months later, Mom said I had to go to Gram's for the summer so that she could move. Marie went to Aunt Viola's, Gram's sister. That summer was awesome. I always had fun at Gram Grover's. I got to go to church and camp again and it was all wonderful spending time with my aunts, uncles and cousins.

I also spent time with another of mom's sisters, Aunt Lillian and Uncle Alferd. They had a farm. I loved the animals, and Uncle Alferd even named one of the cows after me. It was because I had wet my pants sitting on that particular cow, so he named it Barbie. It felt like such a privilege to be the only kid who got away and spent time there. Once again, I thrived during the weeks I spent at my grandparents' farm.

Then I spent two weeks at Grandma and Grandpa Austin's. I loved their farm as well, and it had been a while since I had seen them and they were so glad to see me. And I remember the good times with Gram as we walked down to meet Grandpa on the train. Then we would feed the animals, sheep, goats, cows, and hundreds of chickens. I even watched Grandpa butcher the chickens for supper and it never bothered me, even when they ran around after their heads were chopped off. And it was funny, really, thus the saying, "running around like a chicken with your head cut off." Grandpa told me to think of them as food and not pets.

Gram was a cook at Ken Haven School for years. They made a cookbook using her recipes because they were so good, and the cookbook had photos of her in their kitchen. She was the best baker, and I loved to watch her make pies. Someday I want to go visit there and see the school. My sister Patty takes after Gram. She became a great baker, owned her own bakery and traveled all over the world gathering ideas for her gluten-free cookbook to help people like her. I'm so proud of both of them.

We also visited Uncle Kenny and Aunt Mary, so my cousins and I spent time together. We were all more like sisters since our mothers were sisters and our fathers were brothers. It was just so cool to me. This was another good time in my life! Cousin Linda was older than me and then Carol, then Cindy. My mom's sister, Aunt Evelyn, invited me for a few days to play with Nancy, another cousin. While there, Nancy and I took a container of bubble bath and went down the road a bit to a cool place under a bridge where a little waterfall had formed with a large hole under it. It was waist deep, and we made a big bubble bath. What fun, until someone called Aunt Evelyn. She came to stop us yet couldn't help laughing when she saw the result of what we had done. She finally explained that the soap would kill all the fish. Then we felt badly, and I immediately prayed, "Please don't let the fish die because of us." She shook her head and laughed again.

My visit with relatives completed, it was time to go home again. At least Kenneth H. was still out of the picture. I had heard from my grandmother that he was living in Fort Wayne, IN. He had gotten a job there with a newspaper company. He took Keith and Susan with him, so they all were gone. I didn't have to worry about him being around, but I missed Keith and Susan and felt sorry for them.

[Author's Note: *This was a nice interlude in my life where I felt safe and got to be a kid —somewhat, though I often had to watch the kids for Mom while she worked. Aunt Chicky was staying with us off and on and I loved that. I got to go to church every Sunday with my teacher, but I couldn't get any of the others to go with me, sadly. I heard many Bible stories and I felt like I could relate to a few of them. I joined the Girl Scouts for a year. Life was good but it wasn't going to last. Mom made bad choices that affected all of us.*]

Chapter 6

Another New Start

At ten years of age, I was ready to begin my fourth-grade year in 1962 with Mrs. Sherwin and Mrs. Cassidy as my teachers. My mother had finally left the third story house for a little house near where she worked as a short order cook at the Dudley Diner. ("… ask and it will be given to you; seek and you will find…" Luke: 11:9) I was to watch the kids when Chicky wasn't there until Mom got home. Sometimes I would lead them all over to the diner and the owner would give us all small ice-cream cones.

We were playing on the swing set one day, and a mole was headed for the kids. Some of the boys at school had said to watch out for moles because they would eat a hole through you! I was as gullible as one gets, and I believed them. I grabbed a shovel and ran to save my brother and sisters. I put the shovel on that poor little thing's neck, stood on it and jumped up and down. Mom arrived home and came running over to me. "What on earth are you doing now? Oh my!" She stopped me and sent the kids into the house. Then she helped me bury the mole. I told her what the boys had told me.

"Barbie," she said, "What am I going to do with you? Moles aren't going to eat you. They live underground and are blind above ground. He was lost and trying to find his hole to go home, that's all." I cried a lot. I felt really badly. Then she felt badly. "But you were just trying to care for the kids. You didn't know. It's okay. Just ask me when you're told stuff like that. I'll tell you if it's right, okay?" I answered, "Okay."

With my Aunt Chicky's help, Mom was doing pretty well. Kenneth H. had to pay some money toward the support of Marie and Kendra. My dad still had to pay some child support for me, Brian, and Marie because his name was on our birth certificates. It was nice to enjoy life, mostly due to the absence of Kenneth H. It was a good year. Virginia Kingsbury was no longer four blocks away; she was just one block away. I could go over anytime I wanted. We were still good friends. I was only absent nineteen days that year and tardy thirty.

We walked ten blocks to school. Mom signed me up for Sunday School and I got picked up by Aunt Vi and brought back home. I loved it, but I was sad no one else wanted to go. I won a silver dollar in a contest that year and went to stay with Dad and Sally during vacation break. But there were some rough spots as well. I got roseola and they had me sit in the sun to help me heal. I still was not doing well in school, despite my improved attendance. I was so far behind my peers. Eventually, I spent more time watching the kids because Chicky had to get back to high school; she was graduating this year. *He walks with me and talks with me along life's narrow way*! I sang that song a lot.

My mother met a gentleman, a truck driver named George. My first inkling that something was going on was when he came over to visit a few times. He seemed nice until I saw him slap my mother across the face one evening when I got up to get a drink. I told him not to ever hit my mom again.

"This must be the feisty one." And he asked me to forgive him. He bought me toys and candy after that. He never hit her again, at least in front of me. He liked kids and I found out he had ten of them. I heard him say he would never leave his wife. But he loved my mother and didn't want to stop seeing her. He visited, stayed at times, and gave my mother money to help her out.

So, my mom was able to make ends meet for a while with the money he gave her, along with money from her job, tips and babysitting, and the support checks. During the school year of September 1962 to June 1963, though, she started having money problems again. I don't know the cause, but because of the strain on her finances, she sent me to live with my dad.

I was in Brattleboro for a quarter of the school year of 1962, my fourth-grade year, and I didn't like it. Though I got along with my stepmother most of the time, there were episodes when she was a control freak and was often angry with me. I got the mumps that year, as did Brenda. That caused her extra stress.

One weekend morning, Brenda and I decided to serve Dad and Sally breakfast in bed. We burned the eggs and toast. They both insisted it was good, even though they didn't eat much. Dad could see the humor in the situation and appreciated the gesture. He told us he thought it was sweet and cute. Then Sally had enough and sent us all outside so she could clean up our mess. Dad went to work at the fire station.

We played "hide and seek" outside and Brenda hid under the slide. She stuck out her head quickly to see if I was coming, and a big pigeon flew over and pooped on her head. Tommy and I laughed because it was so funny to us as kids. Sally stormed out and took Brenda in because she was crying. She turned to us and yelled because we laughed. We said we were sorry, but as soon as she was in the house we laughed again.

I loved Tommy. He was fun and so cute. Soon, I had to go the bathroom but I was afraid to knock on the door to go in. So I climbed the fence and crossed the street to ask my friend if I could use her bathroom. I got in trouble for that. Dad said to Sally, "You have to let them in to go the bathroom." They found out Tommy and Brenda both went in bushes when Sally was angry and wouldn't let us in, but I wasn't going to do that.

Sally kept us outdoors anyway. It became obvious she didn't want us in the house at all. She said it was her quiet time to rest. Part way through the school year, a new student entered school. She was seated in front of me and I could see huge head lice crawling on her hair. A huge one fell out of her hair on my desk. I freaked out and ran out of the school screaming, "Bugs! Bugs! Bugs!"

I refused to run to my father's house because it would mean going back to that school. So, I ran to the bus depot and I told them I had run away and I wanted to go back home. Believe it or not, they paid for the bus ticket when I told them my grandparents would pay them back. I arrived in Springfield, VT in the nighttime, and they called my grandparents from the depot. "You got a granddaughter down here waiting for you." My grandparents picked me up, and Gram called Dad. He was glad I was okay and couldn't believe I made it all that way. ("Even though I walk through the valley of the shadow of death, I will fear no evil, for you are with me... Psalm 23:4)

If I had only known what life was going to be like, I would have stayed with my dad. He would have had grounds to get custody. This was one of my bad choices; I seemed to take after my mom when it came to bad choices. Gram tried again to get my mother to let me live with them because I was having such a hard time. My mother wouldn't give them custody and she ended up taking me back with her.

So, I was back again with Mom. I had heard from my grandmother that Mom was living in Saxtons River. It was obvious to me when I arrived that

George was taking care of Mom as his girlfriend. She didn't have a job. Why did she leave the other place when we were doing fine? A man, that's why. Even at the time, I knew it was just another bad choice that affected all of us. Mom always said the only way to survive in this world was to find and please a man and he would take care of you. I believed her most of my life, sadly.

Mom was living in an apartment that was really nice but small. It was an efficiency apartment with two rooms and was in a meadow above the location of George's trucking company. Marie and Brian were with Mom, and Kendra was with Aunt Viola. Now she had me, too, but only because she didn't want my grandparents to have custody of me.

Despite the fact that George was never going to leave his wife for Mom, I began to like him more and more. I was glad when I saw him. I started school in Saxtons River during the second quarter of fourth grade. However, no school record for me exists in that school for that particular time.

It was at that residence where I had my first memory of transgender individuals, though I didn't know it at the time. A guy was living across the street. He was nice to us and often waved when we saw him. Suddenly, he disappeared. No one talked about it, and I didn't understand it at the time. Before long, our neighbor had a daughter we had never seen before, and the nice guy never appeared again. Much later it dawned on me what had occurred, but at the time, it freaked me out. I didn't know if they had killed him or what had happened. We made up all kinds of stories. My suppositions were as crazy as all get out. I still liked playing detective at that age.

While living there, my brother Brian started a fire on the side of the mountain. He said he was just using a magnifying glass to see what the bugs looked like when enlarged. The fire was significant enough to involve the local fire department, and in the flurry of activity, revealed the relationship between George and my mother, most importantly to his wife.

It was just before my birthday. We could no longer stay there, and she had no job or money. Her solution? She called Kenneth H. I couldn't believe it. She asked if we could come there to live with him if she agreed to take care of his kids. Apparently, he had been sending her messages about their nice house and how he was doing better, not drinking. And he would love to have us join him there so he could see his kids.

She informed us we were moving. All I could think about was the birthday cake and ice cream George had promised, along with a special gift, but Mom wouldn't wait. I was so hurt by the fact that she had to leave the day before my birthday.

On November 27, a big truck showed up and packed us all up; they would deliver our stuff, which was not much because Mom had sold most of it when she downsized. We headed to the airport and flew to Fort Wayne, IN. We were told it was a nice place, and it was. It was on Vance Avenue. I went to Rockingham School for the third quarter of fourth grade, another late start, of course. The teacher was Mr. Cavendish, who was my first male teacher.

I didn't do well. I developed more problems with my eyesight. After a few weeks they pulled me out and sent me to L. C. Ward School for the Blind. I was there for the rest of fourth grade and the first quarter of fifth grade. My teacher, Dawn Herger, was my favorite. I really loved that lady; she was so sweet. And I had a friend, Benny. He was totally blind and he sat right next to me. I read to him because he loved to have someone read to him. I had large print books so that I could see the pages. I learned there that there are others who were worse off than I was, and I loved being a teacher's helper for them. *"Take my life and let it be* consecrated Lord to thee!" At this time, it became my salvation song!

Bennie was learning Braille, and I wish that I had learned it at that time, as well. There also were deaf children there. There was one boy named Donnie who preferred to sit in the corner shaking his head. The staff tried to get him to read, and I seemed to be able to sit with him and make a game of pointing at an object and showing him the word. I learned a few sign language words as I worked with him, but I regret that I didn't learn more while I had the opportunity. Even though I loved the school and the students, my brain was still fixated on issues at home. Though I did better there than in most schools, I was in my own little world.

When at home, I spent most of my time outside. I went inside for supper, ate quickly, and promptly went to bed early and was up early. Kenneth H. didn't bother me while we lived at that location. Perhaps it was the too tight quarters with so many of us in a room. He couldn't sneak in and attack anyone, and for that short period of time he wasn't drinking. It also helped that Mom made him get a night job so he was gone when we slept. But there were the weekends.

Just before school ended that year, we all went to the wedding of someone in Kenneth's family. It was the first time we were with his extended family and it was not a great memory for me. We could see why Kenneth H.

was as he was. They drank, swore up a storm, made sexual gestures with their women, patting their butts, and made gross comments about their boobs. It was bad and embarrassing. Even worse, Kenneth's family pressed him to take a drink, which he did. "It's a wedding, have a drink," they persisted. Mom knew what this meant and where it would lead, so Mom decided to go home early, leaving him there with his family.

When we got home, she had me help her pack up everything in an effort to get out before he got home. We packed the roof of the car, the trunk, and the rest of the car until there was hardly room for us kids. She had left Keith and Susan at the wedding party, reluctantly. She felt she had no choice at that time.

We drove back to Vermont. I remember thinking what a long ride. We had taken his car. Mom had taken enough money out of the bank to get settled back in Chester, VT. As we rode along I wondered where we would end up this time. I got to have the back window as my seat; it was not against the law at the time. Brian got the back floor and Marie the other side of back floor. Kendra sat in the front seat next to Mom. I had the best seat since I got to watch the stars, the cars, and all of the scenery. We spent the nights at truck stops. We finally arrived and stayed with family.

[**Author's Note:** *When I look back on this time of my life, I realize I was getting confused on what was right and what was wrong. I started to feel differently about my mother and her choices. She seemed angrier at life and needed me more and more. She couldn't deal with all of us; and she had to make an increasing number of choices that would affect all of us. Life was confusing and hard for her and for us.*]

Not in the fire

Chapter 7

The Orphanage

We stayed with family until Mom found a job and an apartment. She decided Brian and Kendra would go with her to Chester, and Marie and I were going into Kurn Hatten school home for children with a variety of needs, including those in state custody--in Saxtons River, VT. We stayed there for the rest of fifth grade and all through the following summer.

Mrs. Musgrove was my den mother. Since Marie was younger, she was in Hewet 7 with Mrs. Denny, and we hardly ever got to see each other. Marie told me she cried herself to sleep for the longest time.

This was an all-girls home and boys joined us for school and church. Bed time was 8:00 p.m. and we were up at 7:00 a.m. My other den mother was Mrs. Shepherd, who watched us at night. Neither of my den mothers lived there. Marie had a den family with a girl and a boy, both good kids, and that family watched Hewett 7.

I developed a weak muscle in my right eye so I wore a patch for five hours a day for a few months. We were still at Kurn Hatten when I started sixth grade.

Back at Mom's house, the extended family helped her to get by for a while. It was inevitable that she would start having financial trouble, so Brian went to Aunt Viola's during the day and Kendra went to Aunt Hattie's, sister to Gram Grover, while Mom worked. Marie and I were already in Kurn Hatten. It was supposed to be temporary, but we were there for what seemed like two whole school years.

In the beginning, I hated the idea of being sent to an orphanage, as it was known to us, but I didn't hate that place as I had expected I would. There were a lot of girls and we had great fun. I learned to cook, sew, do ceramics, swim better, and I was doing okay in school. A girl named Carol Fresher bullied me and tried to beat me up, but eventually she was removed because she wouldn't stop beating on me and other girls; apparently I wasn't her only target. There was a boy at school named Richard that I liked a lot. He was my second crush because he was so nice to me. But we were just friends. My first crush was in first grade, Danny.

We got to be kids for a change, and, for the most part, I just wished my mother had left us there. We would have done much better. It's not always in the best interest of kids to stay with messed up parents. I had some good friends there. That arrangement lasted so long that Dad stepped up, went to court, and tried to get custody of me. I liked the orphanage, but I really wanted to go with my dad. He was convinced that Mom would never be able to care for us. I told my den mother, who was in charge of our group, that I wanted to go with my dad. I wanted to be with him so badly.

When I made my preferences known, the den mother replied, "If you go to be with your dad, you do realize they will take your mother and lock her up in an insane asylum."

I was so frightened by that. My only experience with what they called an insane asylum was Kenneth's wife. In my child's mind, she was locked up and could never get out. I didn't want to be with Mom, but I cried and cried for fear she would be locked up because of me.

At court, when I went forward to talk to the judge, he asked me to please say who I wanted to live with. When I said, "I want to live with my mom," my dad started crying and said, "What? I thought you said you wanted to come to live with me?" I couldn't look at him. It hurt so much that I cried, too. It was incredibly sad. That was the last time I saw my dad for years and it bothered me for a long time.

The court told Mom I could go with her if she could prove she had a safe house, as well as a husband to support her. She had to settle down and not bounce around anymore. Marie and I had to stay where we were until Mom complied. I went back to Kurn Hatten. Marie was still there, too. Mom made a phone call; she was going to make a life with Kenneth H. if it killed her. That actually was her comment. She promised to marry him and they would adopt each other's kids.

In December, my mother went back to Indiana. She promised she would be back to get Marie and me. I dreaded going back to an uncertain life, though Indiana wasn't that bad before. I liked the idea that I would get to see

Not in the fire

Keith and Susan. I didn't want the name change—yet I had no say in the matter. I trusted God would be with me on this journey and I had to make the best of it.

During the remainder of my time at Kurn Hatten, I saw my grandparents off and on. They were upset that they would not be able to see me as much. I did not see my dad, though; he was too hurt to come and say goodbye.

It was so hard saying good-bye to everyone--my new friends and the teachers I loved, but the hardest of all was saying good-bye to Mrs. Gainin. She was the cook, and we occasionally went to her farm on weekends. She was so nice.

I would not miss the Russian cook who filled in on Wednesdays, only because she would make liver and onions every week. I think she would get a kick out of the fact that I love them now that I'm older. I gave her such a hard time. But if anyone didn't eat a certain meal, they simply got it for the next meal until it was gone. And they got to do the dishes to boot. Wednesday quickly had become my day to do dishes, even if I threw it all up afterwards, I had to try to eat liver and onions every week. It was gross, but I learned to eat my food. In fact, I now eat most anything and I'm grateful to have it.

Everyone took turns setting the table. Mrs. Ward, the dean mother, was strict. If anyone gave the staff a hard time or backtalk, they were given one good belt to the butt. I never had to get that, but I still loved it there, the caring and knowing what to expect, the order, and the rules. It felt safe and nice, and I took all I learned into my future life.

[**Author's Note:** *This was a big turning point in my life. I learned that God loved me and was looking after me wherever I was. I learned to be stronger and defend myself in a different way. I learned that people's comments were not always true and that some adults said things just to manipulate you to do what they wanted. I stopped trusting adults with whom I felt uncomfortable. God gave me discernment. Though there was a brief time when I was afraid, God took that fear away from me.*]

Chapter 8

Adoption

"Trust in the Lord with all of your heart, and do not lean on your own understanding." Proverbs 3:5

Mom was depressed but proceeded with her marriage to Kenneth H. so that she could get us back. They married on February 12, 1965. Indiana and Vermont authorities began working on our reconciliation, and in March 1965 she came back for me and Marie. Then we picked up Kendra and Brian. I had entered the sixth grade in September 1964, so again I was uprooted part way through the academic year. I had a friend, Sharon, and when my mom came to get me I had her hide in the trunk, not thinking they'd be so glad they found her. She wanted to come with me. I saw her many years later when I returned to Vermont. We stayed close for a while, until she moved away.

I found out that Aunt Chicky was coming with us. She was pregnant, by a married man and she intended to live near us in Indiana until the baby was born. Her plan was to give up the baby for adoption. In the end, she couldn't give up Baby Patty. Soon after Patty was born, my grandparents arrived and took Aunt Chicky and Patty home with them. I wanted to go so badly; I missed all of my grandparents.

Kenneth H. ended up adopting all of us on March 5, 1966. The court wouldn't let Mom adopt Susan against her will because she was old enough to make her own choice. Susan wasn't fond of my mother, so she refused to be adopted. Mother adopted Keith. Up until that time, Marie, Brian, and I had the surname Austin on our birth certificates; now we were Kenneth's.

Not in the fire

We started at Bloomingdale School in April after school vacation.

Because of the adoptions, later on, Kenneth H. had to pay child support for all of us. On the flip side, Mom was left with Keith and Susan at a time when he simply disappeared. I found out later that during the adoption proceedings, in order for the court order to be valid, Mom had obtained permission from my dad for the adoption by telling him that I wanted to have Kenneth H. as my dad rather than him. My dad was heartbroken yet again, but I didn't find that out until much later in my life. Eventually, I had the chance to explain the lie, in addition to my decision back at Kurn Hatten?? My dad was sick that he hadn't bothered to investigate it further. We both made mistakes. I told him, "It's over. We just need to let it all go." ("May the God of all hope fill you with all joy and peace in believing ..." Roman 15:13a)

It was about this time that Kenneth H. started molesting Brian. He did horrible things to him that I won't write about. It lasted about eight months. Though it wasn't daily, once is more than enough. I was unaware of this until we were adults and he shared it with me. I cried and felt if only I had known, I would have protected him. Why, though, did I think I was the only one who could protect anyone from Kenneth H? Susan and Keith were abused for years, and I am not sure about Marie, but I assume now that he molested her, too, by how she acted around him. Despite my vigilance on one hand, I just put blinders on to other events. It was more than enough taking care of myself and my mom, though I did watch out for the kids in other ways. I thought the little ones were safe.

I have prayed about why. The only answer I got was a dream of when we were kids and I was the only one who took any interest in church and learning about God. I trusted Him and listened to His "still, small voice." They blocked Him out. We all made choices. Later in life I helped Susan, Keith, Brian and Kendra find Christ and listen to Him; God healed their memories. Though the memories were still there, like mine, the memories were less painful. Kendra was spared because she was just a baby. Marie was not interested in God and she stays away from all of us except Kendra. Sadly, drinking is important to her, just like it was to her dad. She was such a gifted young girl; I was sure she would go to college and be special in whatever she did.

We lived on Case Street in Fort Wayne, about fifteen blocks from Bloomingdale School. We walked to school every day. I got a bike for my birthday that year and I loved it. I rode all over the place with it. Once I saw the boys put their feet up on the handle bars going down the hill, so I tried it. I hit the curb and went flying. I hit a wall so hard it knocked me out for a few minutes. My mom came running. I was glad my bike was okay, but she put it away for a long time, at least until my left knee healed.

I had dislocated my knee and cut it wide open, but Kenneth H. refused to take me to the hospital since we had no insurance. He had been a medic for part of the time he was in the service, so he snapped my knee back in place. Did that kill! He cleaned my wound and only put a lot of butterfly bandages on it, self-made ones at that. I could not go anywhere because I had to stay off it. I hobbled around on one foot. To this day, my left knee is crooked; it makes me walk sideways at times. It's weird, but I've gotten used to it.

I was home for four weeks with the injury and Mom had Keith do my homework for me. That was a stupid decision. School was hard and I struggled anyway but having so much time away from school and no exposure to my school work was a stupid decision.

Then I met Dwayne. He was one of my classmates and I didn't really like him much at first. He was a bully, a joker, and he fooled around a lot. I liked the school that year, but I was so far behind. I had few friends that would come to my house. There was a girl named Linda who lived only three houses down the alley from me. Her parents liked me, so I got to go to her house. She could come to my house, but only as far as my yard. Then there also was a boy named Mark who lived four houses up in the opposite way from Linda. I would go to his house, clean his room and pull him around in his pool, but we were only friends. I wanted to be his girlfriend, but he liked none other than my friend Linda. I gave up on both of them and simply sat in my room playing over and over, *It's my party and I'll cry if I want to.* Oh brother, what a sap I was! I wouldn't go out to play for a while because my heart was broken. It was weird this was the way it would be. ("Is any one among you suffering? Let him pray." James 5:13)

Kenneth H. started drinking again around the holidays that year. He held a large tag sale and sold every toy and all kinds of household stuff so he could buy more booze. What followed were all sorts of other tragic happenings. We were put to bed early so that he could have his steak, lobster and beer without us around. Mom was at his beck and call because she felt obligated to be a good wife.

We all had chores. Susan was in charge of cleaning the house, vacuuming and cleaning the bathroom. Washing dishes and making paper

Not in the fire

bag lunches for school were my responsibilities. Mom did the cooking, laundry and ironing. The boys took care of the trash and cleaning the yard. Marie did the dusting. Kenneth H. found ways to be alone with Brian and Keith. Sometimes it was taking them to his work; the building was adjacent to our back yard. Not only did he molest Brian, but Kenneth H. had this habit of boiling down the printing fluid and sifting it through cheesecloth to extract the alcohol. His addiction prompted him to drink almost anything that could possibly give him a buzz. What's horrible is that he had Brian drink it as well. ("I the Lord search the heart and test the mind, to give every man according to his ways, according to the fruit of his deeds." Jeremiah 17:10)

I caught him, once again in the kitchen, beating my mom. I grabbed a beer bottle and broke it over his head. I simply hated him too much to think about the consequences. Mom's safety was all I cared about.

I hated leaving her to go to school every day, but I had to walk the kids to school. Mom reassured me he was at work. I rushed home every day after picking up the kids. Kendra was the only one home with Mom.

Brian became angrier and angrier. None of us knew about the reasons at the time, but I now blame it all on Kenneth H. Brian was especially mean to Keith for whatever reason, probably because of what he made him do. Not knowing what was going on with him, we all complained to Mother that he should be punished. Mom blamed herself for Brian's epilepsy because it stemmed from an accident. She was protective of him and was afraid to punish him for fear she would cause seizures. Because he was her only son, she was very dotty over him, which didn't help. One day, Mother had enough of our complaining, and he was particularly out of control. She stripped Brian down and took a belt to him in front of all of us. I screamed, "Mom stop it!" He was left with welts all over his back.

She then said, "There! Is everybody happy now? He's punished now forever, for all he's ever done. Are you all happy? I never want to hear another complaint." She never punished him again. I took care of him myself. I was convinced that the marriage had been so hard on her that she herself was out of control. I would just sit on him till he promised to behave. I would do something with him if he promised to be good, like going for an ice-cream. I never wanted him hurt like that again. None of us did.

My mother was not in her right mind. Brian was kept home for weeks until the wounds were healed enough to wear a shirt. I don't know how the school let her get away with his absence, but why did any of our absences go unnoticed? In this case, if they saw those welts, she would have been in deep trouble. I have no idea what Kenneth H. did to him while Brian was home all that time.

One day I came inside from playing with neighborhood kids. As I walked through the door I had just opened, I saw to my right all of my "siblings" were in formation and in hysterics. I turned to the left to see what they were looking at. There was my mother in a chair, and Kenneth was choking her. She was turning purple, ready to pass out.

Without thinking, I picked up a lamp. I bashed him over the head with it. This time, it not only broke the lamp but cracked his skull. Mother dropped to the floor; I ran over to her to see if she was going to be okay. She had marks on her neck, but she was okay. I didn't care what happened to Kenneth H.; I got up, and after checking my mom, I swung around and yelled at the kids, "What the heck is wrong with you guys? There are five of you and one of him! How can you just stand there and let him kill your own mother? Get some spunk in your life for crying out loud!" I was so mad! And they seemed to always come to me with their problems. I was a second mother more than a sister, sadly.

I sent them to their rooms, all crying. Mom got up and she and I dragged Kenneth H. out the back door and left him outside on the ground. Blood was everywhere. We went inside and locked the door. Mom called his boss and told him what happened. Kenneth's boss came and attended to him. Mom called the police, as well; she wanted his abuse on record because she knew that the next time he could kill her or one of us. He did not care for me at all, or Brian, Keith, or Susan, but mostly not me. Not only did he put us in danger, but Mom pointed out that my reaction to his attacks could easily have landed me in trouble with the law. I need to point out, however, that he was the only person in my life I ever hurt. I was not like that. I was brave, but timid, a loner most of the time, and I ran from bullies. What a strange thing.

A restraining order was served on him at work. After he recovered, his boss let him rent an upstairs room on the same property as the newspaper business. He wasn't living with us but he was still too close. Mom obtained separation papers and he was served with them. This was on Cass Street. The timeline of these horrendous events is mind- boggling to me now. It is amazing what children can live through.

These events meant that Mom had to get a job and she took a job with the Van Orman Hotel. She worked as short order cook and waitress for the bar area. The other waitresses covered the tables. I saw firsthand at the Van

Orman how awesome she was as a cook. I wasn't aware of her skills when she cooked at the Dudley Diner. I had been told they hated losing her and now I understood why they valued her so much.

Some days I went by the Van Orman after school and dropped off the kids with Jenny Steiner, a friend of Mom's. Jenny sometimes babysat in her home for money until Mom got home from work. I took advantage of the free time and would go specifically to watch Mom work. The regulars would come in and simply say, "Hi, Flo!" She would respond with a smile. She was happy again and set to work making their regular orders. The waitresses would still respond to the particular table they chose to occupy, but the patrons typically said, "Aw, Flo knows what I want."

I couldn't believe it. They were hardly settled in before their plates arrived; that's why they loved her. She would notice their approach and start their orders. Her boss was nice and he let Mom take home leftover food he couldn't keep. Her customers tipped her very well.

After she'd been working there for three or four months, and still in the middle of divorce proceedings, Kenneth H. started to come over to visit the children. Jennie Steiner felt sorry for him not being able to see his kids, so she let him see them and take them over to the house to visit with them, not realizing the danger she put them in. I simply climbed out of my bedroom window as soon as he entered the house. The first time this happened, I ran all the way to where my mother worked; it was at least two miles. I hid in the kitchen, curled up with my coat as a blanket, under the table out of the way, and slept until my mom got out of work. Her boss said, "Florence. I think your daughter's here."

I told Mom that Jennie let Kenneth H. take the kids over to our house to visit with them, except Brian. Mom called Jennie and said not to do this again because he was abusive to the kids. So Jennie stopped letting him see them. The thing was, he sent everyone to their rooms the few times this happened. He only wanted to see Marie and Kendra. He didn't bother with the rest of us anymore. Susan was starting to stick up for herself and so was Keith, who also began looking after Brian. Finally, they grew backbones. He didn't want to fight all of them so he left us alone.

After this, Mom had a change in her work schedule, and Jennie no longer could watch the kids. I watched them myself. Mom typically got out of work around 10:00 p.m. Then she went back for morning shift at 7:00 a.m. until noon to serve breakfast. I took the kids to school. She was sleeping when we got home. She had a break time to go home to be with the kids, and then at 5:00 p.m. she went back for supper and late shift while the band was playing. I fixed supper for everyone and put the kids to bed. Once they were asleep, I would lock the door and run down the street; Kenneth H had sold my bike a while before. My mom's boss eventually got me a bike so I'd stop running all the way down the street to her work. It was nighttime, and sometimes really dark, but I was not afraid. A particular verse would come to me.: "There is no fear in love…" 1 John 4:18

I was so glad to get that bike, because one time when I ran to see Mom, I stopped on a bridge to catch my breath and rest. I heard a noise by the river, I looked over and, to my horror there was a large dog being attacked by rats, big river rats. They were eating him alive. Seeing that made me sick. I felt sorry for the homeless people that lived by the river. Their fires kept the rats away for the most part, but no one was helping the dog. I ran and never stopped by the bridge again. I told my mom what I saw and she was scared for me. One of her customers heard my story and ran to the river to take photos for the paper. The board of health got someone to shoot all the rats. Amen! Everyone would be safe.

Ronnie Speaks was a singer at the bar where Mom worked and he would often come in to eat before his sho. When I was there, he would buy me ice cream or a milkshake. He called me his pretty young woman. I was flattered. Once he asked Mom if I could stand in front of the door because he wanted to sing me a song. She agreed. I stood on my toes looking through the glass door onto the stage in the barroom. He pointed to me and announced, "This is for my pretty young woman." He sang *Pretty Woman* to me, and then he signed a record and gave it to me. I still have it.

I did not get to go to church and was on my own as far as Bible teaching was concerned while in Indiana. I slept with my Bible all the time. I still had the one Grandma had given me. I talked to Jesus and trusted my life to Hi care. He never let me down. Things happened; it's a sinful world. People make choices that affect not only them but everyone around them, but He is always there to help if you only ask.

Not in the fire

[Author's note: *I believe this is when I started to trust God differently and yet argued with Him about things that were going on. I started to depend on myself more, with no direction from anyone else, because they seemed to depend on me. I took charge of my life and made bad choices as everyone around me had done. They said it was growing up, that everyone disagrees with their parents. So that meant disagreeing with God my Father as well, right? I was getting mixed messages all around me. I was confused in many ways about so much, but I had no one to turn to except God. And I didn't always obey Him. That's called growing up and learning to care for oneself and to be independent, right? It's so sad as I look back! I needed direction to keep depending on God and not myself.***]**

Chapter 9

✦————— ❧❦❧ —————✦

It Takes More Than a Village

Mom started dating a man named Kenny S. before she was divorced from Kenneth H. Kenny S. was in an orphanage and one of about twenty kids. His mom was a local bar prostitute and had a child nearly every year. Among the children were three sets of twins. With each new baby she delivered, she walked to the gate of a Catholic children's home and left the child with the nuns. The Catholic Church raised them all. After my mother passed, I learned that Kenny S. was only two years older than me. Kenny was the fifth to the youngest of all those kids in that same Catholic orphanage.

It was a summer day when Kenny S. and his friend Dino were visiting our home as live-in guests when Kenneth H. came over to the house and began ranting about Mom and her boyfriend when he and Mom were not yet divorced. He pushed Mom around; he was drunk, of course. Kenny S. and Dino took Kenneth H. aside and beat the living daylights out of him as we all watched. Kenneth H. didn't bother us again.

Dino spent most of his time sitting around and playing the guitar. He was quite entertaining to us kids. Kenny's brother Jerry, as well as Jerry's girlfriend Shirley, came to live with us, too. She was also Dino's sister. The whole neighborhood talked about us; and no one was allowed to come over to play any longer. ("… sexual immorality must not be named among you … Let there be no filthiness or foolish talk nor crude joking, which are out of place …" Ephesians 5: 4)

Shirley had epilepsy, yet we didn't know about it. One day she was in the bathroom for a long time. I kept track because I wanted to take a bath before bedtime. Summer school was set to begin the next day. Mom thought summer school would keep me busy and help me catch up with school.

After knocking on the door repeatedly and receiving no answer, I complained to Dino. He was the only one who knew about her medical condition, and he began pounding on the door. He finally broke down the door. He saw her and screamed for help. Jerry and my mom burst into the bathroom. I stood by and watched it all.

Shirley was underwater and they pulled her out. As they performed CPR, there was blood coming from her mouth, ears and nose. My mother noticed me at this point. She shouted, "Get Barbie out of here."

Jerry pulled me into the living room and sat me in a chair. I was in shock. He called an ambulance. Emergency personnel took Shirley away but I knew she was gone. Mom was concerned because I was stunned and silent and stayed that way until later that night. She gave me something to help me sleep, and I did. Jerry, of course, was heartbroken. This was a new kind of horror I'd never seen before. I was in shock and should have been taken to the doctor, like the EMT told my mom.

In the morning, Jerry gave me the new nightgown he'd bought for her, which she had never worn. Shirley had been so nice to me, and I treasured having it as a reminder of her. I wore the nightgown for years until it ripped to pieces. Dino disappeared to inform their family and make funeral arrangements.

It was only a month later when another tragedy struck. My mother developed bladder cancer and had to be hospitalized for three weeks. They decided it was best for her to also have a hysterectomy because the cancer had spread. My Aunt Lillian came from Vermont to help. I loved Uncle Alferd, her husband, but they were having problems in their marriage. I was told it was postpartum depression after her sixth child. My grandparents thought it was a good idea for her to get away from Vermont. Our family was the farthest away and Mom needed her.

Unfortunately, she and Jerry started an affair. He, out of grief; she, out of what I've never been sure. They knew I didn't like it, so they set about to find something to occupy me. Jerry had friends who owned a local laundromat on the block behind our house and he asked me if I would babysit their one-year-old while her mother went out for the evening. I saw the opportunity to earn some money, so I agreed.

I was convinced Jerry was trying to get rid of me when I arrived and saw an older couple sitting at the kitchen table. When I saw how strange they were, I became glad I was there for the baby. I found out later they were the baby's grandparents, parents to the woman who went out for the evening. The grandparents never responded to my greeting and seemed obsessed with some card game.

I fell asleep on the sofa while I was babysitting for the little girl. I do not remember her name. The mom returned from her date with a man who simply dropped her off and left. I sensed he was a nice guy. She seemed nice also. We chatted a bit as she prepared to go to bed.

She had just gotten in bed when another man came bursting through the door. He gave me no thought and went straight to the bed which was in the living room across from the couch I was on. Her parents were still at the kitchen table. I could see them from the couch and they never moved, despite what happened.

An argument started and it soon became apparent that he was her husband. What happened next was horrifying. Her husband stopped arguing and started beating her. Before long, he had his hands around her neck and was strangling her. I jumped up, went into the kitchen and told her parents what he was doing. I was shocked that they simply told me to go to bed. *What is wrong with them*, I thought? "He's strangling her. You've got to stop him," I yelled.

Her parents just prayed and told me to go back to sleep. I was so upset with them. I was wondering what to do, but the "still, small voice" wasn't telling me to do anything but pray, so I prayed, too, *Lord, please help her. Don't let him kill her*. I laid there watching him strangle her until she passed out. He checked to see if she was dead and then darted out of the house. Only then did her parents come in with ice and cold cloths and revived her. She was barely alive they said.

Next thing I knew, they yelled at her, "Next time you will be dead. Go back to him and stop fooling around. You are married! It was your choice to marry him." Then they told her to go to bed and that she would feel better in the morning. They told me she would be okay and I should just go to sleep. *Weird parents*. I asked the young woman if she was okay and I told her I prayed she would live. She smiled and thanked me and told me to try to get some sleep now. She assured me that she was okay and that she was sorry I had witnessed it all.

In the morning she could hardly swallow and whispered she was going

Not in the fire

to see a doctor. Her neck was black and blue and her throat was swollen. She left the house only to return a few minutes later. She was hysterical. She gasped for breath and we finally figured out she was trying to tell us something. We discovered her husband was outside in his car and he was dead.

It finally dawned on them I shouldn't be there and they called Jerry to get me. By the time he arrived, police and other emergency personnel and vehicles had swarmed the place. Her husband had taken a tube, stuck it in the pipe of his car, put the other end in his car window and killed himself. The police saw her neck and sent her to the hospital. They never asked me anything, even though I had stood outside with Jerry and watched it all, including getting the dead husband out of the car!

Jerry said, "It's an easy way to die. He knew he'd spend life in prison because he had thought she was dead." He took me over to Jennie Steiner's and told her, "Barbie can't come home yet, her mom is still in hospital." The kids were all fine, but the beds were all taken. Three of the kids were at Jennie's, despite there being three adults at Mom's house.

Jennie Steiner seemed about seven feet tall. Her head touched the top of the doorway. Her husband was about five feet tall, yet he beat the daylights out of her. I was bold enough to ask, "Jennie, you're bigger than he is. Why do you let him beat up on you like that?"

Her answer was, "Because he's my husband. It doesn't really hurt. He doesn't know any better when he's drunk." *What is wrong with all these women?* I thought. *No one is ever going to lay a hand on me.* I just looked at her and said, "That's so wrong."

I never liked her husband and he stayed away from me. No doubt he heard me holler at Kenneth H. The kids only felt safe around him when I was there. He and Kenneth H. had been friends/drinking buddies.

School was almost over by the time my mom came home from the hospital and I returned to Vermont with my Aunt Lillian. My mother wanted me to go because I had been through too much and had seen too much while she was in the hospital. I was thrilled to be traveling by train. I spent June on the farm with Lillian and my Uncle Alferd, and July and August with Gram and Grandpa Grover. On the train ride, Aunt Lillian had asked me not to mention anything about her relationship with Jerry. Then I spent half of September with my Aunt Evelyn and the other half of the month with my Aunt Chicky and her husband John, who now had their own place in Brattleboro, VT.

I had missed them in spite of their problems. They were both alcoholics, so I babysat while they were drinking. At least they drank at home; they went back and forth between Indiana and Vermont a few times. They would yell and scream at each other, but it never escalated beyond the noise. I loved them but I hated their drinking and yelling. I never could understand why people married people who drank. I remember thinking, *that stuff makes you nuts*! At the end of September, I headed back to Indiana. I took the bus, with a note specifying all of my transfers. I did it by myself with help from the bus drivers; I was proud.

Upon my return to Indiana, I was in charge of taking care of everyone again. School started late for my siblings because of the move to Jefferson Street which bordered a primarily black neighborhood. All I knew about black people was how I sang the song, *Jesus loves the little children,* **all** *the children of the world. Red, brown, yellow, black, and white; they are precious in his sight. Jesus loves the little children of the world!* I had never seen anyone of another color before, so I had no fear or concern. In fact, I was excited to meet God's other children. I had always been at a predominately white school before legislation to integrate the schools. ("O you who love the Lord, hate evil! He preserves the lives of his saints; he delivered them the hand of the wicked." Psalm 97:10)

I entered Jefferson Street School in October of 1966. I found out that I had an astigmatism, and I got a new pair of glasses. It was seventh grade, and the school was fourteen blocks from home. This was during a time when neighborhoods were segregated and there was enormous animosity between ethnic groups. School integration took place that year, and I was sent to a predominantly black school. Another interesting fact about this time was we were not yet allowed to wear pants, just dresses below the knees. Girls only worked at jobs suited for girls and men and boys disrespected girls much of the time. It seemed that girls were looked at as sex symbols. I hated this place already. I found Dwayne Jackson was also at that school. He was the person who was a bully in sixth grade, though he had been sent away due to his bullying. I found out he had been in California with his brother during the time he was away and he got into gang activity while he was there. He came back home tougher than ever and he trusted no one.

The first day at this school, some black students targeted me. I started out happy, and I said "hi" to them all, and told them I was glad to meet them. They thought I was crazy, I guess, and that's why they targeted me. But there was one black girl who was nice to me. She was a big girl, so I ran and hid behind her when I was in fear of the other kids. She told the others, "Shove off and leave the skinny, scared, white girl alone or you will answer to me!" I really liked that girl. They pushed me around a little after that, but eventually left me alone as far as really hurting me. They laughed at me, though, and I was so confused as to why they hated me. I never did a thing to them. I also lacked exposure to that kind of violence in school.

Dwayne heard my voice one day as the white kids threatened to get me on the bus. So I chose to walk home or run if I had to; I was a fast runner back then. They called me a n***** lover because I liked the black girl. My first thought was, *what is a n*****?* Dwayne remembered me from sixth grade. He came over to me and said he would make sure I got home safely. On the walk home, he explained to me what everything was about with the gangs and the ethnic violence. I was shocked. It was an hour later by the time we got to my place because we'd had to avoid the black neighborhood. I thought, *this whole thing is so stupid.* He decided to make me his girlfriend for my own safety once he saw how innocent and naive I was. He said it would look good to his gang to have a girlfriend and it would protect me. Their honor code dictated that if you belonged to one of the gang leaders you didn't get bullied. No one touched a girlfriend that was wearing their colors. So I said sure, but only for looks and my safety.

It worked out for us both for a while and we did become best friends. We could talk about anything with each other. Then one day, Dwayne came to our apartment when Mom wasn't home. She was working and Kenny S. was never around. Dwayne decided I would have to sleep with him or he couldn't be my boyfriend any longer. As crazy as it was, I called my mother at work and said, "He's going to go back to California if I don't sleep with him. If he goes, who is going to protect me? What am I supposed to do?" Her response was, "For crying out loud, Barbara Jean, I've raised you to know what to do. Just do what you know you're supposed to do.

I returned to my bedroom and said, "I'm sorry. I'm waiting until I get married." I reminded him that it wasn't part of our deal. He said, "Fine. I understand." Not only did he leave the apartment, but he also went back to California. Luckily, it was near the end of the school year.

Kenny S. and my mother married on January 16, 1967. He looked a whole lot like Elvis Presley and even wore his hair like him. My mom loved Elvis. Mom played the guitar and we all loved to listen. She was self-taught. Kenny played the guitar, and she loved Kenny. He was good to her. He never hurt her, and he made her feel young, I guess. She said to us kids, "I'm not marrying a dad for you ever again. He's just my husband." But the two youngest looked up to him as a dad of sorts, especially Kendra and Brian.

Soon after Dwayne left, we had a big thunderstorm. It rained for the whole week and the river flooded the street. That caused a flood in the apartment. Because we were so near the river, the water came up to the second floor where we lived. All of the apartments below us were flooded; all the first-floor people were evacuated. We were spared. We were safe but trapped on the second floor until the water receded. When it did, we went out on the streets and had a ball playing in the water. Never did we think about how disgusting the water was, sewage, street debris, dead animals and all. No parent stopped us either. Where's the smarts in that? There are so many parents who either don't care or don't think about the dangers out there. ("But they who wait for the Lord shall renew their strength; they shall mount up with wing like eagles; they shall run and not be weary; they shall walk and not faint." Isaiah 40:31)

[**Author's note:** *This time in my life was so difficult because it was a wake-up call to problems outside of my family. I became aware of so many issues in life that I needed to learn how to avoid. I also saw glimpses of how God was protecting me, and I was listening. God knows all! I learned more about problems other kids endured and that living in the city could present additional hardships. It was different from country life. I wanted so much to go back to my grandparents in the country where there were no gangs that I was aware of.*]

Not in the fire

Chapter 10

My First Job (Besides Babysitting)

By this time, I couldn't do any of the work at school. Keith and Susan did all of my homework because it was way over my head. Keith and I were in the same grade and classroom for years, but I just sat in the back of the room watching and trying to understand what on earth the teacher was talking about. When my mother attended occasional school conferences about my work and my absences, teachers often asked, "Why does Barbara do so well on her homework but so poorly on her work at school?"

Mother told them I was shy, and my brain just froze when I was taking a test at school. She told them it was like a handicap. I thought my mom would be caught in such a lie, but they believed it, as long as my homework was good. My sister Marie only went to school a total of four months a year. She did all her work at home and she got straight A's. It came so easily to her. Yet, she was our family's problem child. She was running the streets and in trouble all the time. That's another reason I believe she was molested. She was having sex at a young age.

It seemed we had just each other for years. We only saw the few friends we made at school. We came home, did homework, ate, and went to bed. On school days, I had to get meals and make sure the other kids got baths and went to bed. I cleaned the house and sometimes soaked Mom's feet for her and wrap them in gauze bandages; she had blisters on her feet that were bleeding at times. I felt so bad for her. She would leave for the night shift and get home at 1:00 a.m. and go to bed, sometimes with tears in her eyes because her feet hurt so much.

I would get up and get the younger kids to school after feeding them and making lunches, which were peanut butter and mayonnaise, tuna fish, or fried eggs. We didn't get free lunches back then. If someone had nothing, they went without. We did get a large block of cheese, flour, and sugar about once a month from the State. I would head to school and drop off the younger kids at their school. I was always late to school and they were accepting of this because they knew I had to drop off younger kids. Everything was in reverse after school. I would pick up Kendra and Brian at grade school. Marie always took off with her friends and I'm not sure what they did with the rest of the day. I had too much to do, so I just learned to let her be. She wouldn't listen anyway.

Keith and Susan would do my homework, then theirs. I could help with the younger kids' homework, which helped me not feel so stupid. Then I'd get supper.

The laundry needed to be done on weekends; we washed it in our bathtub by hand then hung it outside on the line to dry. I made this a fun time. We had an old claw tub. I'd fill it with warm soapy water and then let the two younger kids jump up and down in the clothes. I called it playing washing machine. Ha! Sometimes I'd get in with them and we made a big mess on the floor. Altogether, washing and rinsing all of the clothes took over two hours. They had to drip dry when I placed them on the line, so it took two days for them to dry completely. After they were on the line we would go in and slide all over the wet, soapy floor. Susan and Keith had no interest in this, though. They typically ran off to do something else, like clean bedrooms and take out the trash. Marie never helped do anything,

When the chores were all done I would take the kids out and let them run under the hose to get good and cleaned off. They did all this in their underwear; no baths for them that night. They'd get their pj's on after drying off, and only then would I mop the floor. Mom never had any idea about any of this. She always said how clean the kids and floor were. Ha!

We played a lot of games together. We had no TV for the longest time; that was for rich people, but we listened to the radio. Marie was always sneaking out and when Mom was home she'd be at some friend's house. She picked bad friends. She hated being home. She never liked Kenny S., nor did I, but at least I tried. Things worked out best when I babied him.

Kenny S. would often be out of work. Suddenly, Mom was working two jobs, and it made me sick. He ran around while she worked her tail off. She would get home at 1:00 a.m. and he'd still be out. One time, Mom and I searched for him and found him in the alley with a girl. Mom threatened her. The girl was so afraid of my mom that she never saw him again. This had gone on and on until Mom stopped him from doing it. I had never seen my mom stick up for herself or get mad before this.

In the past, the pattern was that Mom would get two or three months behind on rent and we were forced to leave. She rotated the electric bill, heat and rent through all of our names so that she could get reconnected in each new place. There were six of us, plus her and Kenny's names, so she made her way through each name. When the rent and utility bills got too high, we'd move, and they couldn't find her. I don't know how she got away with it.

Kenny acted like a spoiled brat most of the time. His favorite activity was to sit, eat chips, and drink soda in front of everyone; we weren't allowed to have any. He was lazy around the house and wouldn't work outside of the house. He made messes all over for me to clean up. I didn't care about his excuses; I thought it was terrible that Mom had to work two shifts to support all of us and he wouldn't chip in.

Even I had to get a job to help feed everyone. It was my paychecks that helped my mom get back on her feet. One day, I'd had enough and decided I was no longer going to baby him. I yelled at him, "You're so lazy and a lousy husband! You are supposed to support Mom, not her you!" He was mad and left. He came back with a TV he'd gotten from his family, so the kids loved him. They got interested in watching his shows because it was his TV and we couldn't touch it. Then he started sharing his soda with Brian and Kendra. I wondered if he thought this would make me happier. He'd give Keith some soda if he'd do stuff for him, such as errands to the corner store. A nice older lady owned that store and I used to sweep her floors for a gallon of milk or loaf of bread so that the kids could have lunches. Her name was also Florence and she died before we moved away. Again, I was sad. She was a great example of another hard-working woman.

My job was the second shift at Abdow's Big Boy, after the kids went to Jennie's for her to watch them. This was fifteen minutes away from us at the time she needed the extra money to feed her kids. I took a bus across town to work and back. Sometimes Kenny S. agreed to pick me up me if I got him free food.

It was at that job I met a guy named Leo. He was one of my customers and he paid me particularly good tips. When I met him, he was in his senior year of high school, and as the end of the school year approached, he wanted me to go to his prom with him. I asked my boss if he knew the guy or anything about him. I explained that he had asked me to the prom. My boss said Leo was a nice young man and had a nice family. I agreed to go. Mom was happy I had a date with a nice young man, so she took me to a used clothing place where we found a nice, long yellow dress.

On the way to the prom, Leo took me to meet his mom and dad. They were nice and they were short like Leo. I had never seen him outside of his car, so it kind of shocked me. It brought to mind Jennie Steiner and her husband. I always thought they looked awkward. Dancing with him was weird. His head came to my chest. I sensed his friends were laughing at us, as well. It didn't seem to bother him, but it did me.

He was so nice and fun, too. When he dropped me off at home and had to stand on the step to kiss me goodnight, it was even more embarrassing to me. When I went into the house I found everyone at the window, laughing. The next time he called, I told him nicely it wasn't going to work out. I reassured him I had fun, but we couldn't date. I explained it wasn't his fault, but I didn't want to get serious yet with anyone. It was among the most ridiculous decisions I ever made.

The crazy thing was that his brother was in the service and wrote me a letter asking me to reconsider because his brother really liked me. I wrote back to his brother to explain my reasons for not dating Leo. His brother's name was Gary. I understood he had the same problem with girls because he was also short, but he wondered if I would be a pen pal and would be happy if I would just keep writing. I did and we became good friends.

When he got out of the service, he came to meet me and gave me a gift he brought from Vietnam. At that point we said goodbye. He was taller by only a little and he knew how I felt about height, so he never tried for more of a relationship. He moved on in life and wished me well. He had become like a big brother to me, so I missed him, but we never talked again after that visit, sadly. I started a different job that summer.

For several summers, Mom shipped me off to be a nanny for a lady and her three sons. My mother, Kenny S., and the kids would show up every payday and collect my paycheck; Mom would leave me with five bucks and then disappear. On my one day off a week, I was allowed to go roller skating, and often it was with Kenny S. That was Kenny S. The one thing he liked to have fun doing was skating and he was a good skater. I am not sure how he learned to skate while at the orphanage.

Sandy Niemeyer, the mother of the three boys I watched, was nice to me. I loved the boys and I loved working for her and her husband, who was

Not in the fire

a truck driver. I enjoyed living with them all summer. I often wished I could have lived with them full-time. The boys liked me, too, which was good. They could be tough at times, but most of the time they were good enough, and the youngest was my favorite. He was such a sweetie. I had to return home during the school year to help with the kids, and I also resumed working nights at Abdow's Big Boy.

[**Author's note:** *During this time I witnessed many hurtful things. I know God helped me to get through it all. I worked at being brave and independent. I learned basic survival skills. I was looking around me all the time watching out for trouble, yet I wasn't fearful at all. I tried to be bold yet caring of others. I was growing up fast and dealing with things I shouldn't have had to deal with.*]

Chapter 11

Unfortunate Witness

Soon after the flood on Jefferson Street, Mom decided to move to a new house was on St. Mary's Avenue. It was a nice house and she had a deal with the landlord to fix up the place and her rent would go toward purchasing it. She was so excited. While she got the house ready for all of us, I and my older siblings stayed at Jefferson Street.

On one of my days off from work, I decided before I moved I would say goodbye to an elderly lady who had helped me out in a number of ways. I had no idea that the most traumatic event I ever have witnessed was about to happen. It occurred as I was walking through one of our old segregated neighborhoods. As I walked down a particular street, I noticed a commotion that I decided to explore. The street was full of people and the crowds seemed to be segregated by color.

In the middle of the commotion was a young, pregnant woman of color and a white man. The couple was tied to a tree. I overheard that it was the parents of the young couple who had tied them up. One of the parents yelled, "We're not going to have any half-breed babies. You both will be an example of what happens when blacks and whites date."

These people proceeded to cover the couple with gasoline and set those young people on fire. It was beyond belief. I'll always remember the screams. As soon as I saw them on fire, I ran fast toward the apartment. I heard the screaming for blocks. I was sick to death about it; it haunted my sleep for a long time.

I went to my mother's, still in hysterics, and told her what I had seen. She looked at me in disbelief but said she would check into it. She found out it really had happened. She warned me to stay out of it and to tell no one what I had seen. I never went to that part of town again. That is when I developed a discomfort around black people. I thought the same thing would happen to me if I associated with someone of a different color. ("For there is a time to be silent and a time to speak." Eccl. 3:17)

Chapter 12

A New Home

It was nice to finally have a home to call our own on St. Mary's Avenue. Mom painted a mural on one of the walls and had worked hard to fix up the place. It looked nice.,

Rather than have to answer for how little I attended school and explain the discrepancy between my homework and my performance at school, Mom decided to withdraw me a few months into my eighth-grade year, and I had only done school work to get me to below average seventh-grade work! This is when she declared, "The only thing you're going to be good at in this life is being a wife and mother and taking care of people, or maybe cleaning. You don't need school for that. I need you at home."

I had to get the kids up every morning for school and then I would clean the house. After this, I had some time to myself. I kept in touch with other friends who were in school. I had to quit my job because they began using roller skates, and I could not serve food on skates. Mom made Kenny S. get a job as a bell boy where she worked and made him start giving her money so they could buy this house. It was about time! I found out later that Kenny S. couldn't read or write, not even his name. It was so sad that he was worse off than I was.

I remember Mother returning from work one day so tired that she didn't want to see the house as it was and screaming at us for our latest activity. We had pulled all our mattresses from the bedrooms and lined the stairs with them. What a wonderful slide they made! I thought it was highly creative on my part. I cleaned it all up when Mom came home.

I needed extra money so I agreed to babysit for a single woman with two kids who rented from Jennie Steiner, our former neighbor with the abusive, drunken husband. I asked if my friend, Linda, a girl from my old neighborhood, could join me. I hadn't seen her for some time. They agreed that she could help and we would share the money. We spent the night, expecting the mom to return early in the morning.

At eleven that night there was a knock. There were two young men at the door who said they wanted to see the mom. We never should have opened the door, and they took us by surprise and pushed their way into the apartment. One of them said, "We're just going upstairs and wait for her."

We were nervous and couldn't go to bed with them there. They were hanging out, talking, laughing, and sputtering among themselves. Eventually they said, "Do you have anything to drink in this place?"

I served them some soda, and we had some too. They started watching TV at about the time one of the kids became restless. Apparently, while we were checking on the kids, they put something in our drinks. We didn't realize what they had done.

We both started feeling woozy and then downright ill. Linda wanted to go home so one of the guys offered to walk her home since she wasn't feeling at all well and only lived a block away. I found out later that he had raped her. She became pregnant from that attack. Her mother put her in a Catholic home until the baby arrived and then put the baby up for adoption. I never saw Linda again, but I heard her parents kept her from anyone other than their Catholic friends after that.

Meanwhile, back at the apartment, the other guy tried to attack me as well. I was sitting on the sofa, which was at the top of the stairs that led to the exit. He pushed me down and tried to take my pants off while sucking my neck. I repeatedly told him, "No!" I tried to fight him off. I was groggy and he was heavier than I was. Nothing I did was effective, but I kept praying, "Lord, help me!" He just laughed at me, "He's not going to help you!" Then the "still, small voice" said to me not to worry, help was coming.

All of a sudden, this guy came to the door. He heard my screams and broke down the door, flew up the stairs, and yanked the attacker off me. He threw him down the stairs and yelled, "What the **** are you doing? Get out of here! Do you want to go to prison for rape?" My rescuer seemed to know the attacker. ("The Lord is my rock and my fortress and my deliverer." Psalm 18:2)

I was worried about my friend and told the person who rescued me about the guy who had taken Linda home. He said he would look into it in the morning. He helped me wash my face and put a cold compress on my throat. He put a mattress on the floor and stayed close as I cried myself to sleep and eventually passed out from what had been in my drink. He stayed until the mother came home as promised. He was a friend of hers. They called my mother and Kenny S., who both came to get me. My mother could see I was still woozy. She told me to say nothing more of it, and Kenny S. would take care of it. I never knew what happened to those two creeps. I had to wear turtlenecks for weeks, but I came out of it so much better than my friend. I thought, how do I deal with this? I'll tell no one. It's between me and God.

Dwayne and I had resumed our friendship; things were so on and off with us. I still loved to ride around in his convertible. We would go to a drive-in movie or anything, since I just wanted to get out of the house, even if it was with Dwayne, and Marie loved his friend Chuck. This was a short period of time when Marie would listen to me and we got along. One evening, Kenny S. let Dwayne and Chuck into the house without our knowledge. They came upstairs into our bedroom. I was sleeping in the same room with Marie because Chicky and her two kids had been occupying my room and her stuff was still in it in case she came back.

Dwayne climbed into my bed, held his hand over my mouth, and forced himself on me. I had fought as long as I could, telling him, "No! I don't want to do this!" He said, "Don't scare your sister; Chuck is sleeping with her!" Marie didn't seem to be resisting Chuck, and I was exhausted from the struggle. So I quieted down. I regretted that for years.

I don't know where my fight went because I just cried when he finished. I told him I never wanted to see him again. My dreams were crushed. Gram had convinced me the one who gets you first is the one you have for life. **But she didn't mean like this, did she?** In any event, the notion stayed with me.

Marie loved Chuck and didn't seem to care about what he had done. She didn't get pregnant because Mom had gotten her birth control pills to help with her painful periods, and because she knew Marie slept around. I believe this was from what she experienced while being molested by her father. In my family, nothing was spoken about sex. It was part of life and it was assumed we would do it sooner or later. Kenny S. had said, "All you girls need is to get laid, and then you won't be so cranky." He was so wrong. And who gave him the right to make that choice? My mom would have had a fit!

Chapter 13

War Time

I was friends with a young man we'd met who had been informed he would be drafted. He was shy and sensitive and I met him through Dwayne and Chuck. We all hung out together spending some time with my sister Marie. His name was Craig and he was two years older than I was. Marie was three years younger.

Craig had a brother, Mark. I was surprised when Marie left Chuck for Mark. We were also introduced to another friend of theirs named Steven, who died in Vietnam; we all went to his funeral. His youngest brother Leo joined the army and lost his life in the war, as well. We all became close to his family.

It is because of those deaths that Craig was so scared when he got drafted. He was sure he would be next to die. He was shy and passive. He talked about it with me often. He came by one night to chat and was sitting at the end of my bed crying his eyes out about his fears. He had been avoiding the draft notices and he was sure they were coming to get him.

Sure enough, there was a knock on the door and I heard my mom's voice, as well as other voices I didn't recognize. I knew it was the military police. I sprang into motion. I pulled my bed from the wall where there was a storage door, almost like a trap door. In there was an old rug. I took it out, unrolled it, and rolled it back up with Craig inside. I shoved it back into the storage area. Then I moved the bed back in place. It sounds like quite a production, but I did it in a matter of minutes.

A soldier came up to my room and knocked on my door. He asked, "May I come in?" I said, "Sure."

The soldier asked, "Have you seen Craig lately? I know he's your friend.

Someone told me he hangs around here."

I said, "It's been a while. Craig said he was going to Canada."

The soldier looked around and said, "Yeah. I guess there's no one in here." Then he saw the trap door. He asked, "What's in there?"

"It's a spooky hole. I keep my bed in front of it so I don't have to think about it." He responded, "Well, I need to look in there." He moved the bed and checked it out. ("Though I walk in the midst of trouble, you preserve my life." Psalm 138:7) He opened the door and peered in using his flashlight. He saw the rug and kicked it to see if he could get a sound out of it.

There was no sound, and the soldier said, "Naw. There's nobody up here." As he left, he turned around and said, "We're going to be watching this place. We've been told he hangs around here with you, so if you see him, it's in his best interest if he turns himself in."

I said, "He's my friend. He doesn't want to be drafted. He's running because he's afraid."

"Well, I can't help that. He's been drafted. That means he has to go." I said, "It's just not fair."

He said, "Life isn't fair, girl," and he left. As soon as I was sure they were gone, I got Craig out of there. He was nauseous and turning purple. He lay on my bed, and I shut my drapes. I fetched him some milk and cookies to help calm him down. When it was completely dark, he climbed out my bedroom window. I gave him one of my old outfits so he would look like a girl. I dropped him down by tying my sheets and blankets together. He was caught eventually and drafted into the Army. He never served overseas. Several months into his service the Army decided to discharge him because he was useless to them. He moved to Canada. I never heard from him again.

There was always noise at night from somewhere in the neighborhood. One night, there seemed to be an unusual amount of noise and commotion from next door. The next day, which was a Saturday, when the laundry was washed, I took the kids out back to play while I hung up the wet clothes. Suddenly, police were everywhere in the alley so I sent the kids inside. Of course, I had to see what was happening. I snuck up to the bushes and separated them so I could see on the other side. Ambulances soon arrived, as well as more police cars.

When I asked what was going on, he gave a standard reply that it was just a routine wellness check, but it was obvious something had happened. I managed to move for a closer look and I was sick. The mom and the three kids were covered in blood; all of them were dead with their throats slashed.

I went back to my house and was sick to my stomach. I wouldn't let the kids outside. I only told them the neighbors were dead. The newspaper reported the next day that the ex-husband was jealous and had killed them all. He told the police if he couldn't have them no one could. He was found on the run and went to jail, reportedly for life. The neighbors were such nice people and of course I was so sad, especially for the kids.

When I told Mom she read the paper and asked, "How much did you see?" After I told her she just said, "Oh, Barbie, you're just too inquisitive. It'll only give you lots of nightmares." I never did have nightmares about it. I prayed God would let me sleep and He did. Once the guy was found, we let the kids go out back to play, but only if someone was watching them.

Though I was only sixteen, I left home shortly after that and got an apartment of my own; even though it was a hard decision, I was tired of helping my mother. Kenny S. needed to get a job; he had lost the bell boy job because of not showing up, so he started working as a busboy in the kitchen at Mom's hotel so she could keep an eye on him. Mom said he could keep his tips but he had to use the rest to help the family. She wasn't going to support him forever. Good for her!

I lived in a sketchy end of town. It was rumored there was a rapist on the loose. Convinced by my grandmother's words that I would always be tied to Dwayne, I let him hang around again. He tried to help me out and one way he tried was by giving me a dog, but he was just a puppy; it became apparent a little Saint Bernard puppy wasn't going to do me any good for a few years, and then he would be a big Saint Bernard in my tiny apartment. It just wasn't going to work.

The apartment was full of cockroaches. I slept with all of the lights on, which I hated, and I hated everything else about that place, as well. One horrible night, someone broke though the downstairs door. I assumed it was the rapist. The intruder tried to get in my door, and I thought he was going to succeed. I stood at the door with a knife to defend myself if he got in, and I prayed for God to intervene. Then I heard Dwayne come in the front door. I yelled to him, and he came running up the stairs. He chased the invader down the back stairs into the alley. When Dwayne finally returned, he told me not to worry. He said the guy would never bother me or anyone else again.

I packed up what little I had, took the dog, and asked to move back with my mother. I told Mom what happened, that I was sorry for leaving, and she let me come back, but the dog had to go. Dwayne found a farmer who took the dog. I was home and helping out again, but at least Kenny was working. They found the rapist dead a few days later, just down the alley from where I had been living. It made me wonder, but I said nothing!

Mom and Kenny gave me my old room back. Chicky was living there also. She had left her husband, who was getting abusive. As usual, the house was full of people. She had to room with the other two girls, Marie and Kendra, and with her two kids. Good thing it was a large room.

Not in the fire

Chapter 14

Another New Home

The family had been in the St. Mary's Avenue house about two years when the landlord came by, as Mom had arranged. When he saw how nice the place looked, he realized, *Wow, I could get lots more money for this place!* Mom had put lots of money and time into that home and had worked hard fixing it up, and we had lived there about two years. Never in her life did she fix a place up again! After he left, he sent us a letter that we had to move because he had decided to sell the house. Even though there was a verbal agreement to sell it to us, he decided he was going to sell it right out from under us. Mom was so hurt and mad because we had to move, and it wasn't because of bills this time. She had put in so much time and effort to keep this place. Her big mistake was never getting the agreement in writing. This time we were going to be moving to Cass Street and our deadline was October. This was in 1968, a little bit into my eighth-grade year. I felt so bad for Mom. The landlord told her she got rent cheap for two years for fixing up the place. He was sorry, but this was business. I learned a big lesson from this: always have everything in writing.

Eventually I got a job with the animal shelter and an apartment of my own over the local laundromat. It was on the other side of town by where we started. I got enough to pay for two rooms. The neighborhood was okay, and I loved my little pad. I had a mattress on the floor and had lined up boxes on their sides to make a dresser. After covering it with a cloth, I put a lamp on it. There was a bathroom with a tub with a skylight over it. I could look up at the moon and stars, and I could relax, be alone, and say my prayers. ("I will instruct you and teach you in the ways you should go; I will counsel you and watch over you." Psalm 32:8)

My next job, for better pay and full-time, was three blocks away at a Catholic orphanage. The Society for Prevention of Cruelty to Children had found the job for me, and it paid more than the animal shelter. There was a little girl there named Tonna; she was attached to me and I to her. Her mom was a single mother and also worked two jobs, so she entrusted her daughter's day care to the orphanage until she got out of work.

One time I was pushing Tonna on a tricycle and went too fast. Her leg got caught in the tires and it snapped her ankle. I felt so bad. She had a cast on it for the longest time. I got permission from her mom to take her home with me once in a while. She was so cute. I wanted a little girl just like her someday. She gave me this cute little doll to fix for her that was made of cloth. It was all worn out. I told her I was going to name my first daughter after her.

But there were secrets I discovered about that orphanage while I was there. The structure was an unusual construction with many catacombs underneath the building. Often I would sneak into the catacombs for some alone time. I learned a great deal on those explorations. Things were going on that were not right. ("So then, as we have opportunity, let us do good to everyone ..." Galatians 6:10)

There were bedrooms in the catacombs and there were trash buckets with used condoms in them. I began to understand why fat nuns disappeared only to reappear months later, yet skinny. It was obvious to me they were pregnant. There was a section of the orphanage that was rumored to house the babies born to nuns. It was beyond my comprehension.

Then one day I was going down to the catacombs to look around and I overheard the nuns talking about Tonna. They were planning to take the mother to court and get the little girl taken away from her because she supposedly didn't spend enough time with Tonna. I understood her predicament. She worked two jobs and had to sleep some time. *What a horrible thing to do*, I thought. I told my mom about it, and she gave me the number of a good lawyer who was inexpensive.

The lawyer would need a down payment. I prayed about it and that "still, small voice" told me what to do. The next time I saw Tonna's mother I gave her the information and half of my pay check to help her with the lawyer. I offered to be a witness if she needed me. The nuns had no idea what I had done at that point, but about a week later I was washing the dining room floor when the head nun came in and told me I was fired. She told me just to leave the floor as it was, with suds all over it. She gave me my last pay

Not in the fire

check and said, "Just leave and do not come back." I got up, got my stuff, and left; I knew why she fired me. I looked at her and said, "I am sorry but what you guys were planning to do was wrong." She just frowned and said to leave.

The next day I went to my gynecologist. A friend saw me there and told Dwayne he had seen me at the appointment. I had started feeling sick and went to get checked out. The doctor said I was four months pregnant and I could not believe it. I was 17, not married, and having a baby. I was terribly upset.

Dwayne came over to my apartment and asked if it was true. I said yes. He wanted to do what was right, and my grandmother's voice rang in my ears, *Once you've slept with a guy, you belong together.* So I thought I was stuck with him. Getting married that way wasn't what I had in mind, however.

With no job, I didn't know what I would do. Then my mother and the whole lot moved into my little apartment; they didn't ask, they just knocked on the door and moved in. I didn't want to stay there any longer. It was so crowded and not mine anymore. So I let them have it.

My mother was not happy when she found out about the pregnancy. She took me to Dwayne's house and told his parents what their son had done. His mother had the nerve to ask Dwayne if it was true. My mom was furious. Dwayne stepped in and said, "Mom stop it, she doesn't sleep around. I know it's mine."

His mother then said, "Then you're going to get married and move in with us." Mom said she didn't want me to marry him, she just wanted them to make him pay support and she would take the baby as hers and Kenny's, since she could not have any more kids. I said, "No way!"

She was so mad. So we moved in with Dwayne's mother and father. They wouldn't let us sleep together. I didn't care. I didn't want to sleep with him; at that point, we had not seen or talked with one another for about four months. I cared most for his dad, his dad's mother, and some of the other family members, but his mom was mean-looking and never smiled. She was dangerously overweight, and she talked to her dead mother at night—actually had tea with her. It freaked me out.

It was then I found that Dwayne believed in Satan worship. I hated it. I could only imagine what my life was going to be. I cried, "Help me Lord. Please!" His paternal grandmother was a quiet old lady and was a Native American. She advised me not to take any guff from Dwayne, saying, "You take this broom and hit him over the head if he doesn't mind you." Dwayne laughed it off. He loved her. I told his grandmother he was going to help me get back to Vermont so that I could be with my dad. I had called my dad, told him how I was and all I had been through, and that I missed him. I asked, "Could I please come home?" He said, "Yes." He was so sorry. ("For if, because of one man's trespass, death reigned through that one man, much more will those who receive the abundance of grace and the free gift of righteousness reign in life through the one man, Jesus Christ." Romans 5:19) Dwayne had a visit to a so-called doctor friend that helped people who had no insurance. This friend supposedly exorcised evil spirits from children. I was horrified and thought he was molesting the children instead. Many of them had problems with bleeding after their "sessions," and parents noticed. The "doctor" justified what he was doing by saying it was the spirits leaving them. They were all frozen, in a state of shock, when they left. It was at that point I told Dwayne I wanted to leave that environment for good. So we left.

[**Author's Note:** *Despite being surrounded by people and events that were an affront to my beliefs, I still believed God would help me through the bad impact of other peoples' choices—especially those in which we had no control. I grew stronger, yet angry, at life. I wanted to go to war, fight back, perhaps be like Florence Nightingale, and help the poor wounded soldiers.*]

Not in the fire

Chapter 15

Back to Vermont--at last

During the short time I lived with Dwayne's parents, I happened to bump into the nephew of Kenneth H. I had seen him a few times over the years, and he was now married and seemed glad to see me. He invited us over for supper. I can say that he was one of the few nice family members.

When we arrived for supper, he served pizza while we chatted. He asked me how everyone was. I told him how hard it was for Mom to raise us all, including Susan and Keith. I told him his uncle hadn't paid support for years and explained how his uncle had abused me when I was younger and how I hated him.

He surprised me. He called his father and asked for his Uncle Kenneth's phone number. Then he called Kenneth H. and told him that he needed to send me some money to get home to my dad's. He explained that I was pregnant and married and that he owed me that much after the hellish life he put us all through, including abandoning his kids. I was shocked that he agreed to send me $300. He claimed that's all he had.

In May of 1970, Dwayne and I were married by the Justice of the Peace. We finally had enough money to go to Vermont, so we packed the car and headed for my dad's.

Dwayne promised when we got settled and he got a job, he would pay Kenneth H. back. We didn't want to owe him anything. About three months after we arrived we drove to Kenneth's apartment to repay the money. I started to feel sorry for him. He seemed so old and crippled up. It was sad. What a waste of life, and it was all due to booze. I couldn't see how it was worth it. He said he was sorry he was not in a good place back then. I said, "It doesn't look like you are now either, I'm afraid." He shook his head. I said goodbye and started to leave. Instead, I turned and said, "I forgive you. God says we need to forgive." And I walked away and never went back. ("Fear not for I am with you...for I am your GOD. I will strengthen you; I will help you ..." Isaiah 41:10)

I hadn't seen my dad Lloyd for years. He and I had a long talk when I returned. I explained what the den mother at Kurn Hatten?? had told me would happen to Mother if I chose him instead of her. I explained that I never asked Kenneth H. to adopt me and that I wanted nothing to do with him; to emphasize how I felt, I even explained how Kenneth H. had molested me. I told him everything, how he had abused many of us. By the time I finished, Dad was in tears. It was sad, but finally we were reconciled. He said he knew he should have fought harder.

Sally and I made peace with one another, as well. She genuinely wanted to be there for me. I understood she had been through a great deal in her life, as well, yet she wasn't as angry as before. All of my half-siblings and step-siblings were still living at home at this time.

It was a full house, so Dwayne and I lived in the camper trailer in the back yard. Dad had hitched up the heat since it was October and starting to get cold. By November, Dad found an apartment for us and helped us move. I loved that cute little place. We had a stove from Dad's workplace at Suburban Propane. I liked the kitchen because it had a little pantry where I could make bread and pies and do all of my baking. There was a large living room and the bedroom was off the bathroom, but we didn't care. It was our own place. To the extent possible, we were happy there.

Dwayne as my husband never quite felt right, but I thought it was the only way to keep my baby. We both tried to make the best of it. I was having his baby, and he was trying. I was thrilled to be a mother, exactly what I always wanted and was best at, but I wanted it under better circumstances.

My grandmother had a baby shower for me and my cousin Ronnie's wife, Ellie, during the fall months before Tonna was born. My mother was back by then. She had been kicked out of the apartment that had been mine and decided to follow me back to Vermont.

Gram said to me, "Barbie, you go make up with your mother. She's your mom." I started to say a negative comment and she stopped me and said, "I don't want to hear it. You forgive and that's it!" I never talked back to Gram, so I did what she said. Mom started talking to me and she would

Not in the fire

call once in a while. Gram had the "talk" with my mother also.

I enjoyed getting to know my sister and brothers on Dad's side. It was wonderful seeing Gram and Grandpa Austin and all my cousins, aunts, and uncles. I was with Dad for a few months before and a few months after Tonna was born, which was on January 2, 1971. A few hours after Tonna was born, Dwayne came back to the hospital to visit and showed me his draft papers. He was one year older than I was. He was supposed to leave the next day. Dad worked with the draft board to get him into the National Guard instead. He left for six months of basic training.

I was happy at Dad's, but at night I was lonely. The kids had their friends and everyone was busy most of the time. I had no friends; Mom didn't work, so it seemed the best thing to move to Perkinsville near her.

***

Sally and Dad were sad when I told them I was moving to be closer to Mom and Gram. Tonna and I moved in April to a mobile home in Perkinsville, VT. *What was wrong with me?* Another stupid move in my life. It would have been so different for us if I had stayed with Dad. After that, my life got continually worse.

After basic training, Dwayne came home. He was glad to see Tonna, but he knew we didn't have a relationship. I didn't want to sleep with him. I never wanted us to be more than friends. He helped me move into Westview Apartments, a genuinely nice place. This move represented a full circle in my life since it is where Mom and Dad lived when I was born. Dwayne stayed a short while before we decided it wasn't working for either of us.

Soon after that, Dwayne went back to Indiana to his folks. He had not seen them since we left. Then he joined the army. I filed for divorce shortly after. I had been baptized in the Advent Christian Church of North Springfield where my grandfather was a founding member. Because of the divorce, the Advent Christian Church removed me from membership. I was devastated and it upset my grandmother. I was allowed to attend, but unless I was going to reunite with Dwayne I could not be a member. ("I will uphold you with my righteous right hand." Isaiah 41:10b)

I remain convinced the marriage was a mistake and never should have taken place. Yet because I was underage I knew that the state of Indiana would have taken Tonna if I hadn't married Dwayne. It was state law that and adoption by the family or the state would take place if you were under 21, unwed, and had a baby.

A friend took me for the final decree of my divorce in the most slippery winter weather one could imagine. The court had a last-minute opening, and I took it as a sign the Lord was preparing the way for my divorce.

On our way home from Montpelier to Springfield, we crossed a bridge and the car spun out on the icy surface. We had prayed before we left the courthouse, and that still, small voice prompted me to reach over and touch the arm of my friend who was freaking out as the car whirled out of control. Calmly I said, "Let go of the wheel and lift your foot off the brake."

I said that just as we crossed the bridge and the car was headed for an aluminum rail with a steep ledge just beyond the rail. When she relaxed her hold on the steering wheel and lifted her foot off the brake, the car slid to a stop right beside the rail. I remember looking over the ledge and thinking, *that must be at least five hundred feet down.* If we had gone over we surely would have died! As I prayed, a "still, small voice" said, *Your life is spinning out of control much like the car--I have calmed the car as an example of your life—give it to me and life will work out better for you.*

We sat there praising God, and slowly started for home. We had no more problems along the journey; He was with us and we needed not to worry. My friend became a believer. It was so cool. We remained friends until she moved back to Pennsylvania.

[**Author's Note:** *I look back at this part of my life and reflect on how my life could have been better if I had stayed in Brattleboro with my dad. Yet how can one know that? I took the bus to visit him. My mother still depended on me and I wanted to be near my grandparents. I did a lot of good, so that is where God wanted me. My bad choices were not His fault.*]

Chapter 16

Independence

We were in the mobile home a short time when I knew I had to move away from my mother into a better place. That's why I chose Westview. It was within walking distance of the store, so there was no need to depend on anyone for rides. It had two floors and included two bedrooms; it was nice. Because of a rent subsidy, the payment was reasonable and included utilities and heat. With a little help from state assistance, such as food stamps, I was finally able to take care of myself. I really enjoyed that but I wanted to someday be free of welfare. So, I started testing for my GED. After six months, I passed and with good scores. ("... with God, all things are possible." Matthew 19:26)

I had been at Westview seven months when Mom, Kenny S., and the kids got a place directly across from me. Theirs was a three bedroom. It was no surprise that Mom continued to depend on me; besides, Tonna was her only granddaughter. Add to that, my Aunt Chicky and her two kids moved into the apartment next to Mom. It didn't bother me as much because I loved my aunt.

There also was an old man, along with his wife, daughter and sickly mother, who lived on the other side of Mom's apartment. He was enormous. I guess it was difficult for him to bathe because he smelled terrible. His wife and daughter were mentally challenged. My mom did a lot for them and he paid her with cigarettes. This relationship will become important later on in the story.

For a little extra money, I obtained a job with the local council on aging. I was on the board and attended all of their meetings, so it actually paid off having Mom close, since she was able to watch Tonna. I even wrote a change that would positively help the elderly. Through involvement on the board, I found out there was a job taking care of folks in the housing project. I got the job and I was able to take Tonna with me. My clients loved her. They watched her play with toys while I cleaned for them. She could come with me when I shopped and ran other errands for them, as well. I walked everywhere, including the store at the base of the hill and downtown, as well. I loved this job, except when a client died.

Susan and I actually became friends of a sort. She dated a nice redhead, and I liked him. She had a job and an apartment, and ultimately she became pregnant. The boy's mother told her he was never going to marry her. It was a horrible thing for his mother to do since they were devoted to each other.

Susan was so shocked when he dumped her that she aborted the baby. My mom had not offered her help and I could barely care for myself and my daughter. I didn't see how I could help, but now I wish I had. It has bothered me all my life. She started drinking after that and started going out with only girls again. She died of what was called consumption a few years later. ("Do not judge and criticize others, so you may not be judged, criticized and condemned yourself." Matthew 7:1)

My cousin, Lee, Aunt Vi's son, came to visit with me several times. I had saved for my first car, which was a blue Chevy. It was used, but I loved it. I was fixing it up--inside and out--while I worked on getting my driver's license. One day, when Lee came by and said he wanted to help me, I asked, "Do you know how?" He reassured me he did. So while he put in my new battery, I finished cleaning the inside of the car. He hollered he was done and for me to turn it on to see how it sounded. So I turned the key. It sounded so good. I got out and while we were looking at the engine there was a sudden boom. The car burst into flames, and I ran to call the fire department. They came and put the car fire out. They claimed the battery had been put in backwards! I was so mad at Lee. He turned red and said, "I'm so sorry. I thought, how hard can it be to put in a battery?" He disappeared and never offered to help me pay for a new car. His parents yelled at him, but that didn't help me. I didn't see him again for three years. He just couldn't face me. We made up eventually, and soon after he was diagnosed with cancer. He didn't live long after that, unfortunately. It was sad he left a wife and children behind.

I worked hard for another year and got a VW wagon, a red one. I loved it. I had learned to drive a go-cart, so it felt like a go-cart to me. When I was

Not in the fire

younger and Mom was married to Kenny S., he loved go carts. Once I got the car, I made a lot of friends. Everyone needed a ride or wanted to do something fun. I finally had a way to go swimming at the pond and other fun activities. The car represented freedom to go more places and see other family members. I was able to make frequent visits to all of my grandparents, as well as my dad.

I was also dating again around this time. I had a lot of dates with nice guys, but the relationships never worked out. In all honesty, it was mostly because of me and my distrust that anyone really could care about me. In the back of my mind, I kept saying, Ya right. It won't last! I now think a few of them could have been long-term boyfriends if I hadn't been my own worst enemy. I was told no one wanted a ready-made family, so I was doomed. During this time I also started helping others around me who needed help or just needed a break--especially watching their kids. It was fun.

[**Author's note:** *I never had a boring life. Through writing down my memories, I sometimes wondered how I endured. These events cover a fraction of what I lived through. GOD is the only answer. My insecurities drove many of my choices at this point in my life! Maybe "Mr. Right" would have come into my life if I had trusted God, but insteadI listened to people at church telling me which portions of scripture to read. I should have listened to the still, small voice that I had let fade, and I went through more than this book could ever hold. My whole life has been one thing after another.*]

Chapter 17

Helping Others

"By this all people will know that you are my disciples, if you have love for one another." John 13:35

Another encounter that led to more adventures happened when I made it a point to pursue a conversation with a young lady I often noticed while on routine errands. I spotted her several times, and more than once she was with a man who was abusive toward her. They lived in a tent on the hill across from the church. I found out Lauri was only fifteen years old and was with this guy, a drug dealer, and she was very ready to give birth.

This particular day, I observed him leaving and decided to park at the bottom of the hill, walk up, and introduce myself. I asked if she needed anything. She started crying. I asked her if she really wanted to have a baby in that tent. She said she was scared and afraid of him. She said he planned to sell the baby for money and that she had no one to help her.

I said, "Yes, you do, me. Get your stuff. You're going home with me." She said, "Really?" I said, "Yes. Let's go." I took her and her little bag of stuff and took her home with me. I gave her Tonna's room and moved Tonna in with me. I made her stay inside for her own safety.

Her boyfriend found out where she was and came by my apartment. He demanded that I "give her to him." I just said, "NO! She doesn't want to be with you, so you can leave now or I'll call the police." He left but said he'd be back. I told him, "Thanks for the warning. I'll be ready."

He left at that point. In the middle of the night we heard the window in the kitchen break. I told her to stay put. I took my baseball bat and went down the stairs. I turned the light on and I heard the door slam. I went into the kitchen and saw that there was flour all over the place. My rent money was kept in a plastic bag in my flour jar, and it was gone! I called the police and they arrived with lights and sirens. They followed the flour down the hill and into the woods. They found my canister on the ground and kept going until they found him covered in flour. They couldn't find the money, however, and they assumed he had hidden it somewhere. He claimed there was nothing in the jar, but he went to jail for breaking and entering. It was his fourth time, so he got a three-year sentence. A few days later, Lauri delivered a baby girl, Jennifer, and she was a cutie. They stayed with me for two months, after which Lauri said she wanted to go home to Hartford, CT., where she grew up.

We purchased bus tickets with some help from a local church. I wanted to go with her, and I left Tonna with my mom. (*He walks with me and talks with me along life's narrow way.*)

When we arrived in Hartford, Lauri wanted to search for a friend to tell her she had returned and was safe. This friend's brother was a drug dealer, so Lauri wanted to be cautious about connecting with her friend. She simply wanted her friend to know she was okay and had a baby girl.

All of a sudden, she ran back to where I was waiting across the street from her friend's home with the baby. Lauri was crying and said, "Well, I said goodbye, let's go." She looked back and said, "Oh no, they're coming. I owe her brother money, and I don't have it."

I calmly took hold of her and said, "Hold the baby tight and close your eyes." I reached over and touched her hand and the three of us moved close to one another. ("…ask, and it will be given you…" Luke 11:9) I told her to look down, stay still, and watch God take care of us. I often stopped and prayed while on an errand for my mother if a car stopped and seemed menacing, and that's what we did then, as well. I simply prayed in Jesus' name that He would make us invisible to them. We stood perfectly still. I could see the car out of the side of my eyes and could hear them talking, "There were two of them and a baby. Where did they go? I saw them."

They were not far from us. One answered the other, "I don't know. Maybe you've had too much to drink." The other snapped back, "No! They were right here!" Then we heard the car drive off. I said to her, "Now you can open your eyes." She waited a moment, opened her eyes and looked around, "That was incredible!" ("...present your requests be known to God..." Philippians 4:6)

"You know, Lauri, with God, all things are possible. You have to have faith that if you ask He'll do it!" I had learned that as a child. Anything we ask in Jesus' name is given to us, but we have to ask and believe it will happen when we need His help. We can't just demand "things." He is God. It has to be for a really good reason and not a selfish one, nor anything not in His Word. He never contradicts His Word.

Sadly, I can't walk by faith for other people. As we left she said, "Now what? We have no money, where will we eat supper and stay for the night?" We prayed and asked God what to do. I thought of the Salvation Army.

We had supper there and they provided clothes and diapers for the baby. They put us up in a hotel for one night and gave us money for breakfast the next morning. She said there was another friend she could call. The friend invited us for lunch and let us rest for a few hours since we had been walking around while deciding what to do.

We walked some more after leaving the place where we had lunch and stopped at a church that looked open. We used the bathroom and decided to stay there for the night. Our thinking was that it's God's house, we should be safe there. We fell asleep on the pews.

Then the pastor showed up and he asked us if he could help us. I explained our situation, and he said he would put us up in a hotel for the night, but we couldn't stay in the church. After a good night's sleep and breakfast, he drove us to her mom's door. We thanked him.

Her mom was far from excited to see her and said, "What are you doing back here? And with a baby. Are you crazy? Your dad will have a fit. We can hardly feed ourselves and your brother and sister. We're not feeding you and your baby. You just can't stay here." She slammed the door in our faces. I could hear her dad hollering, "Who was that?" Her mom said, "Just a salesman. I sent them away."

So we left. I asked Lauri what she wanted to do. I offered for her to come back with me or stay there. She wanted to stay with people she knew, so we found another church and, once again, I asked for them for help. They made it possible for her to obtain an apartment someone in the church owned. We spent seven days painting it, gathering furniture donations from members at the church, and getting her settled. I took her to file for welfare, food stamps and WIC. She also settled into the church and seemed to be doing well.

It was time for me to go home. I missed Tonna and I had a return trip ticket, so I headed home. I was happy to be home and praised God for all He got us through. ("Seek good, and not evil, so that you may live…" Amos 5:14a)

It was only a few weeks later when someone from the bar where my cousin worked said, "You're not going to believe this. Lauri's back. She's down at the bar." No! I immediately left for the bar to confront her. "Lauri, what are you doing?"

"The landlord tried to rape me, so I walked away and left everything. I got a bus ticket here."

"Why didn't you call me?" I asked.

She said, "After all you did for me, I didn't want to bother you with it. And I thought you would be mad." I told her I was mad, but not at her.

I called the pastor at the church and let him know what had happened. He didn't believe her story at all. "Well, it will be a long time before we help anyone again," he said to me after I said God wants us to help others in need. "Was she supposed to stay and continue to be abused? Listen, people have bad times and good times. You don't give up on everyone forever because it doesn't work out the first time. Most of the stuff in the apartment belongs to parishioners, so be sure they get it back if they want it. Besides, think about the fact that the landlord tried to rape her. What would you suggest she do?

She knew you wouldn't believe her, and she was right, since you don't!"

He then apologized and said he hadn't realized the circumstances, but he had a hard time believing it. I also apologized and thanked him for the attempt to help.

So she stayed with me. One day, the housing people sent a guy over to paint the place. They were great at keeping the place looking nice. The guy's name was Bob. He painted for the housing project and he spent a good deal of time with the baby, Jennifer, and Lauri. After a while he fell in love with Lauri. She was flattered that he liked her and Jennifer. They liked the same things, and she grew to also love him.

After just five months, he proposed. I was happy that I was able to attend their wedding. Eventually they moved to Florida where his family lived and he got a job as a carpenter. About four years after they moved, I received a letter thanking me for helping them. They had four children, including a set of twins, and another on the way. They said they attended a nice church. I choked up when I read that. They were happy in a home of their own. I would have loved to have been more involved in their lives if they hadn't

Not in the fire

been so far away.

There was a young man who was so cute, though he was too young for me, who also needed help. He had been kicked out of his parents' apartment, and I found him walking around one chilly, fall night. I invited him in to have a cup of coffee. I knew his family since they all lived in the housing project, but Bobby had issues with his dad. I couldn't send him out into the cold so I told him he could sleep on my couch. He ended up staying with me for a few months.

One day his sister came over and said she had permission from her husband for her brother to stay with them. He would have to share a room with his nephew. He was okay with that. They didn't have much, and I told them I would help her. I gave her $30 of my food stamps every month for a year until Bobby got a job. I even went back to the church that helped Lauri and told them how that went and asked if they could please help Bobby. He needed some dental work. He had really bad teeth that caused him lots of pain. The church in Springfield, VT set it up and paid for it.

[**Author's note:** *This was a trying time for me. I had mentors to help me grow in the Lord, but I still clung to what I knew best--***the still, small voice of God***. I didn't wantto lose that. I honestly thought people had no idea of my reality. So I prayed God would open their hearts to His voice as well. I didn't understand how anyone could survive by onlyreading and not the interaction with His voice. We need both! I wanted to help others to read and listen.*]

Not in the fire

Chapter 18

The Hospital Adventure and More

Soon after, I got a job at the Holiday Inn. It was an evening job and my mom watched Tonna. There was a cute guy who was staying at the Inn while in town working on construction. I was a waitress and served him supper a few times and agreed to go out with him.

He had a Harley, and we had so much fun. I really liked him and asked if he'd like to stay at my place instead of paying for the hotel. He said he'd like to, but he had a boa constrictor. I said it was okay with me, as long as it stayed in its tank. He said if I watched it while he was working, he would pay me, so I did.

My mother showed up at my work one evening to tell me Tonna was at the hospital and not doing well. She had gotten into a box of moth balls. I was so upset. I let my boss know I was leaving and on the way to the hospital. Mom picked me up and explained she went outside for a cigarette. When she went inside, Tonna was on a shelf eating the mothballs saying, "Popcorn."

Kenny was supposed to be watching Tonna but was too occupied with his TV show. Mom felt horrible, but I was so upset I couldn't talk to her at that time. She dropped me off at the hospital and I went in to the emergency room. Tonna had to have her stomach pumped and an IV was in her arm for a blood transfusion. She was so sick. I stayed at the hospital with her for a week before I could take her home. I quit my job and went on welfare again. I didn't think I would ever leave her again until she was older. She could only eat baby food until she was five years old because of this; it messed up her stomach so badly. My friend started to pay board and a little extra for watching his snake. We were close and I grew to love him. The day came, of course, when his job was over and he planned to go home to New York. He said he was sorry and would miss me and Tonna. I was so sad. A week later I found his phone number on my phone bill and I called him. His father answered and said he wasn't home because he was at his bachelor party. He was getting married. I said never mind and hung up. I was shattered and cried for days.

I decided to buy myself a boa constrictor because I missed his boa. Our family doctor, Dr. Moteri, came for a routine house call and saw the snake. He could not believe it. I displayed him in schools to show him off. The time came when he got too big and I could no longer keep the boa. He could get out of his tank and would curl up at my feet in my bed or get into the springs of the couch. I kept Tonna's room door closed at night, but that was not enough. I called a Native American friend that always liked the snake and I asked if he'd like to have him. He was overjoyed and made him a closet room with a glass door so he could have more room and see what was going on. That was the end of the whole adventure for me.

I got a job cleaning tables at a snack bar that was part of the VA Veterans Center. I trusted Mom with Tonna again. I thought she would be more careful. It was a part time job, and Tonna was three years old. I got good tips. The bartender was also a golf pro. He was nice to me and we started dating. I had high hopes that it would lead to something real, but after coming home and meeting Tonna a few times, he began to feel more attached than he had planned. He decided it had to end before it went too far. He had plans for the golf circuit, which did not include a wife and child. So he ended our relationship, and I quit that job. Heartbreak once again.

A few months later, a friend asked me to date her friend's brother. I agreed and we had a good time. I asked him over for supper one night. I was surprised when I got a call from, guess who? His wife! She had heard about his involvement with me. I was so angry I decided to invite her to my place on an evening when he was expected for dinner. I told her the time to be there, which was an hour before his planned arrival. She agreed to hide in my kitchen broom closet. When he arrived, we kissed and sat down to eat. He proceeded to say sweet comments about me and how much he liked me. I arose, walked to the broom closet and opened the door. He was stunned and his mouth dropped. His wife told him off, and he said, "I can explain! Let's talk about this." They headed toward the door and she turned around and thanked me. I was so mad I refused to date again for a year or so.

My mother introduced me to her friend's son, Robert. My mother and his mother accepted gigs together in bars playing guitars and singing. I was

Not in the fire

hoping he was someone I could be with. I was shocked when he chose instead to date a local drug addict named Kora. After they married, they moved next door to me.

He and Kora had a daughter and they named her Vita. I agreed to watch Vita during parties they had at their apartment. I also agreed to watch children of other parents who attended the parties. I was aware of the drug activity and felt I was helping to keep the kids out of the scene and safe while they slept in an adjacent bedroom. It became a job. I needed the money and I could protect the kids. Tonna stayed with my mom.

One night, at a different apartment, I was hired to watch the kids. After the kids were asleep, some of the partyers asked if I wanted a soda. I didn't realize they thought it would be funny to put acid in the drink. I freaked out. I began to see things and when they told me what they had done, I left and intended to go home; I ran as fast as I could. Luckily Tonna was with Mother that night also.

I stopped for help at my friend Joanna's apartment, where she lived along with her boyfriend and her son, Sean; I often babysat for Sean. They helped me to my apartment. I had never felt that way before; I wondered what would happen to me. I prayed and asked God for help. I decided to lie on my couch, and I heard that still, small voice telling me I was going to be all right. Then He told me to call a friend, my mechanic at the time. Mickey was upset but told me to stay on the phone so he could help me. He told me to relax and he'd tell me a story and to not hang up. He started telling me of Alice in Wonderland and that she was on an acid trip. As he spoke, the story came alive in my head. It seemed so real and it was cool and scary at the same time. By the time he ended the story, he told me to go to sleep. I did and when

I woke up, I had a bad headache and was sick. I called my mom and told her what they did to me. Mom called Robert's mother and Robert's mother called Robert and chewed him out. I never baby-sat for the partyers again.

Though I had nothing to do with their parties after that, I was still concerned for the kids. Their parents' drug involvement only got worse. One day I heard Vita fall down the stairs next door and I went over. I wondered if Kora had pushed her down the stairs because she was so high on something. I told Robert and he had Vita checked out. She had a broken arm. Kora frequently was high and never remembered what she did to or with Vita.

Not in the fire

Robert got angry at times over her lack of care, along with everything else, and they often fought. Sometimes he left her but always returned. They were restless and gave up that apartment, only to move back into another one in the complex a short time later on the other side of me; thus, I heard their racket from another angle. And I was still aware that the baby wasn't cared for as she should have been. She cried much of the time.

Eventually, Robert told his wife he wanted a divorce. She didn't argue because she didn't want to be married anyway. He kept Vita and his wife moved in with Franny, a nice kid. Franny fell in love with Kora, and she introduced him to drugs. In the end, Franny decided he didn't like the drugs and wanted no part of them. So she left him. He was brokenhearted. He wanted her to stay but to stop taking drugs. He hung himself in his barn. His family was devastated, as were many others.

Robert got drafted. He asked me to watch Vita during his three-year obligation, and I agreed. Vita became like a sister to Tonna. Robert didn't want Vita with his mother or with Kora, but he wasn't attentive to her either. He rarely visited when on leave. Kora didn't care as long as she could take Vita to get food stamps and then she willingly brought her back to me. A baby only cramped her life. She did visit, and I tried to help her turn her life around. She didn't want to. Vita called me Mom and called her own mom, Bad Mummy. Kora would look at Vita and say, "You're right. I'm the bad mom." Kora told me again to keep her. And I did. For three years. And Robert's mother, as strange as it was, never asked to see her granddaughter.

[**Author's note:** *I dated no one for a long time, in fact, for at least three years. I helped kids and the elderly, had cleaning jobs, and I grew closer to George, Nancy and their kids. I volunteered at church food pantries, readily accepted the free food they provided, and grew to love and appreciate the pastors. I rededicated my life to God during this time and was baptized again.*]

Not in the fire

Chapter 19

Making Friends

Joanna, the friend who guided me home the night of my acid trip and lived in an apartment nearby. She became a good friend. Joanna also had a brother, Joie. He visited often and asked me out for coffee on several occasions. I think he was interested in me, but I didn't see him in a romantic way. Joanna introduced me to four other young women, and we all got along. They didn't do drugs but they did drink.

We all went to dances together. Given the alcohol abuse all around me growing up, I was determined not to drink, though alcohol was a significant part of the dancing scene. I just wanted to be with my friends and have fun dancing. It had been years since I had real friends. After a while they got me to drink just one drink. I would limit it, but I just wanted to fit in. I wasn't listening to my "still, small voice." I argued, *I'm fine. I'll be fine. Don't worry.*

Our group would meet other friends of Joanna's as well, and we all had a pact that no one would ever leave alone with a man. Despite that, one of the girls in our group who had been drinking too much left in a van with a group of guys one evening. We got into the convertible of one of my friends and chased after her. The guys in the van saw what we were doing and tried to get away from us, but they couldn't. They finally pulled over and dumped her out on the side of the road.

We picked her up and found that she was pretty beaten up. They hadn't molested her. It was a scary experience, especially for her but it didn't stop us from having our fun every Friday night.

One of the bartenders showed an interest in me. His name was Larry and he often offered to buy me a drink. It was nice not to have to pay. He introduced me to a new drink, the Shirley Temple. He said if I didn't want to drink, he wouldn't put any alcohol in it and no one would know. So I did that most of the time, but I did have a coffee brandy once in a while.

One evening while I was dancing someone spiked my drink. I don't know who. I felt sick and went into the bathroom to throw up. I passed out on the floor. Two guys burst in and picked me up by my feet and arms.

They carried me past an outside bar, not the one where we danced. They took me to my car and drove me home. They walked me all night long. They made me drink lots of milk, which I never did because I hated milk. I threw it up in a bucket and they gave me more. I did not recognize these guys, neither do I remember their faces. ("Are not all [angels] ministering spirits sent to serve those who are to inherit salvation?" Hebrews 1:18)

I was so tired. Finally I was allowed to lie down on the couch and go to sleep. Before they left, they reassured me that when I awoke I would be alright, even though I would be sick for a few days. They recommended I stop going to the bar. It was almost supper time when I awoke and went to my mother's to pick up Tonna. She insisted that I tell her what happened, and I did.

She was furious. "You shouldn't go down there. You're going to get killed."

As I left her apartment, the old guy next door to her called me over to his window, "What were you doing last night? You had the lights on all night walking in circles!"

I told him about the guys helping me. He said, "I don't know what you're talking about. You walked in there by yourself. I watched. There were no guys in that house. You were walking around the house drinking milk. I couldn't figure out what you were doing drinking all of that milk."

"You're kidding me, right?" I asked. He insisted, "No! There was nobody there but you." *Wow! Thank you, God, for your angels to save me! I'll never forget nor will I go back down there.*

I am convinced that two angels dragged me out of that bar and took care of me all night. I knew He was telling me to straighten out my life and to listen to His voice again. To be sure, I asked everyone to tell me what they saw. My friends were wondering where I went after I left for the bathroom. They saw me leave alone. I was bent over, but they saw no one else.

I stopped going out with those girls and partying. I did not want to lose my daughter and my mother had reminded me I could. I remained friends with Joanna and watched Sean when she went out; but that was it. She eventually moved into her boyfriend's place, which was not a good thing. He

Not in the fire

was addicted to drugs. It was during this time that an individual known as Nelly, who actually flashed the red light to show she was available, along with her girls, lived across from me. There were customers in and out of her place at all hours. I felt bad for her because she was socially ostracized.

One night I was at a different bar across the street from the one where I had partied. My cousin owned this particular bar. He told me I'd be safe there and I could play pool. I needed to get out, and there was nothing to do but go to bars around there. One evening Nelly came into the bar to get a drink, and she was already drunk from the bar across the street where I used to go dancing. My cousin had a temper and he lost it when he saw Nelly. He told her, "Get out! I don't want your kind in my bar."

She was very drunk and refused to leave. "It's a free country. I can go anywhere I like." And he said, "If you don't get out, I'm going to punch your lights out." He pulled back his fist to punch her, and I bounced out of my seat so fast and, without thinking, jumped in front of his hand. His fist hit my hand. He yelled, "What on earth is wrong with you? I could have hurt you." I yelled right back, "You cannot hit a girl! What is wrong with you, Dicky?

Get your temper under control. You can't punch her lights out! She's drunk and she doesn't know what she's doing." He shouted back, "Then get her out of here!" ("If anyone is caught in any transgression, you who are spiritual should restore him in a spirit of gentleness …" Galatians 6:1a)

I felt sorry for her. I helped her out of the bar. She never went back there again. She sent me a nice thank you card saying that no one ever stuck up for her or cared for her like that. I sent a card back and told her, "The Lord says we have to take care of each other." I followed up with information on becoming a believer, but I confess, I don't know what happened to her. Her red light was taken down a few months later.

I started dating again and this time I tried to choose just the nice ones. I was so lonely. I wanted a husband so badly, but I believed no Christian man would ever give me a chance. Typically, after a few dates the fellow would say,

"Sorry but I'm not really up for a ready-made family."

It amazed me how often Tonna would act up in front of my dates or dump food all over them, or even wet her pants. They would not be heard from again. Some would say how much they liked me, but that it just wasn't going to work. Some said that if I wouldn't "put out," they would leave. I let them leave. I wasn't going there again until the right one came around.

My mother introduced me to her friend's son, Robert. My mother and his mother accepted gigs together in bars playing guitars and singing. I was hoping he was someone I could be with. I was shocked when he chose instead to date a local drug addict named Kora. After they married, they moved next door to me.

He and Kora had a daughter and they named her Vita. I agreed to watch Vita during parties they had at their apartment. I also agreed to watch children of other parents who attended the parties. I was aware of the drug activity and felt I was helping to keep the kids out of the scene and safe while they slept in an adjacent bedroom. It became a job. I needed the money and I could protect the kids. Tonna stayed with my mom.

One night, at a different apartment, I was hired to watch the kids. After the kids were asleep, some of the partyers asked if I wanted a soda. I didn't realize they thought it would be funny to put acid in the drink. I freaked out. I began to see things and when they told me what they had done, I left and intended to go home; I ran as fast as I could. Luckily Tonna was with Mother that night also.

Then he told me to call a friend, my mechanic at the time. Mickey was upset but told me to stay on the phone so he could help me. He told me to relax and he'd tell me a story and to not hang up. He started telling me of Alice in Wonderland and that she was on an acid trip. As he spoke, the story came alive in my head. It seemed so real and it was cool and scary at the same time. By the time he ended the story, he told me to go to sleep. I did and when I woke up, I had a bad headache and was sick. I called my mom and told her what they did to me. Mom called Robert's mother and Robert's mother called Robert and chewed him out. I never babysat for the partyers again.

Though I had nothing to do with their parties after that, I was still concerned for the kids. Their parents' drug involvement only got worse. One day I heard Vita fall down the stairs next door and I went over. I wondered if Kora had pushed her down the stairs because she was so high on something. I told Robert and he had Vita checked out. She had a broken arm. Kora frequently was high and never remembered what she did to or with Vita.

Robert got angry at times over her lack of care, along with everything else, and they often fought. Sometimes he left her but always returned. They were restless and gave up that apartment, only to move back into another one in the complex a short time later on the other side of me; thus, I heard

Not in the fire

their racket from another angle. And I was still aware that the baby wasn't cared for as she should have been. She cried much of the time.

Eventually, Robert told his wife he wanted a divorce. She didn't argue because she didn't want to be married anyway. He kept Vita and his wife moved in with Franny, a nice kid. Franny fell in love with Kora, and she introduced him to drugs. In the end, Franny decided he didn't like the drugs and wanted no part of them. So she left him. He was brokenhearted. He wanted her to stay but to stop taking drugs. He hung himself in his barn. His family was devastated, as were many others.

Robert got drafted. He asked me to watch Vita during his three-year obligation, and I agreed. Vita became like a sister to Tonna. Robert didn't want Vita with his mother or with Kora, but he wasn't attentive to her either. He rarely visited when on leave.

Kora didn't care as long as she could take Vita to get food stamps and then she willingly brought her back to me. A baby only cramped her life. She did visit, and I tried to help her turn her life around. She didn't want to. Vita called me Mom and called her own mom, Bad Mummy. Kora would look at Vita and say, "You're right. I'm the bad mom." Kora told me again to keep her. And I did. For three years. And Robert's mother, as strange as it was, never asked to see her granddaughter.

"Lord, will I ever get a husband?" I had been troubled but prayed that there was somebody out there who wanted a wife and a child. When Robert finally came home for leave, and we spent time together along with his daughter, I thought, **maybe this will work out**? I thought I was falling in love with him and I thought he loved me. He asked me if I would get a visa and come to Germany to be with him since he planned on two more years in the service. I was thrilled; I obtained a visa and was ready to go. He wanted me to bring his daughter and Tonna with me.

My mother decided to double check with Robert's sergeant through Kenny's brother, who was in Germany at the time, to make sure everything was legitimate with Robert. I'm glad she did. We found out he was dating his lieutenant's daughter. He knew I was coming yet he hadn't said anything about the other relationship. In fact, he said he had a place for us.

Needless to say, I stayed in Vermont. I continued watching Vita. It wasn't long into the third year of his enlistment when he had to marry the lieutenant's daughter because she was pregnant. The lieutenant sent them both back to Vermont.

I was furious about all of it, but most of all because he never came by to talk about getting his daughter. Even worse, his mother showed up at my door demanding that I give Vita to her. Supposedly, the request came from him, but I did not know if that was the truth and tried to resist her. She showed me a paper she had with her and she said, "If you want me to bring the police I will." I felt I had no choice, and she took Vita. Vita had never met her, and she was scared to death. I was angry and sick about it.

Looking back, I never should have given Vita to that woman. Robert was furious and told me, "Why did you give Vita to her? I would have given her to you!" ("But one thing I do: Forgetting what lies behind and straining forward to what lies ahead," Philippians 3:13)

Even though I could wash my hands of Robert and his mess, it was still devastating. Vita missed me and she cried on the many nights I called to see how she was doing. She said she missed her momma and her sister Tonna. I would say her prayers with her on the phone. I tried to convince her that they were her real family and they took her away from me. I tried to get her back with me through the Department of Social Services, but to no avail. It was a horrible time. I tried to comfort her, but there was nothing I could do. The calls subsided, and the next time I saw her--I ran into her in a store--she spit in my face. It was heartbreaking to know that my beloved four-year-old hated me. I never stopped praying for her.

[**Author's note:** *During this time of "singleness," I enjoyed the girls, took them to church, and spent time growing closer to Ronnie and Claudia, Melinda, and a few other friends from church. We enjoyed picnics and field trips, and I saw families as they really should be. I became cynical about my own family. Yet, God met my needs in amazing ways. At different times, food and money were left at and under my door; I had not told anyone my needs. I pulled away from most of my family except my grandparents, and my dad.*]

Chapter 20

New Beginnings

I obtained a job at the local library and soon worked as the children's librarian. I loved it. Not only was it fun, but I also got a good paycheck. Along with some assistance such as food stamps, I was paying my bills and doing well. We still had a cute one-bedroom apartment with a backyard.

Around that same time, I was out for a walk with Tonna and I met up again with George and his family. George's family treated us as though we were part of their family and we spent a lot of time together.

George was Greek and looked like an Old Testament prophet. He was loving and kind. He had a wife and three children and he invited Tonna and me over often. Being part of their family made me wonder what it would have been like if he had been my father. Besides the frequent meals, they took us places. They were such good friends and stayed a part of our lives for years. They helped me to get over losing Vita and see it was for the best just to keep her in prayer. In fact, George and Nancy were relieved when I no longer had to care for Vita, even though they knew how concerned I was after I relinquished her to her grandmother. I tried again to get her back through the Department of Social Services, but I didn't succeed. I knew the head person and he felt my being involved with a troubled family would not be good for me. Ends up, he was correct, yet as you'll find out later, God used me in a different big way!

The pastor of the Baptist church, Aulbrey Jones, and his wife were really cool, as well. (He died of cancer years later.) I had friends I could hang with, I became involved in Bible studies, and I could take Tonna. I felt like a new person. I rededicated my life because of their influence. The pastor's wife and I sang together, *Take My Life and Let It Be*, and it was reflective of what was happening; I meant every word of it. I didn't feel my life was for me, but for Jesus. My main focus was taking care of my daughter and myself; I wasn't obsessed with a husband any longer.

I gave up hope of someone to love or of being loved. In fact, I didn't feel as though anyone would ever love me. I have always been so passionate, loving and romantic, which I valued as great gifts. I knew so many women who were abusive in their relationships and spent much of the time under the influence of alcohol or other drugs. So many husbands remained devoted to these women. I always went out of my way to be the best God would want me to be. It sounds strange, but my mother said, "If you find someone that cares, he'll provide for you." I wasn't sure I ever would. My life was in God's hands.

So I gave up and focused on doing something useful with my life, mainly helping neighbors. George tried to help me see life with greater hope and to understand that still, small voice in a different way, a bigger way. Because of George's influence, I became a member of the Southern Baptist Church in Springfield, Vermont. Another couple, Claudia and Ronnie, also went to this church and we became friends at this time and are best friends, even to this day. I believe that is when things started to pull together for us. George, who was a school teacher at Springfield High School, knew I wanted to become a model, so he had his shop at school set up a photo lab. He and his wife and the kids did a bunch of photos of me for a portfolio. It was fun to work with them on this project and we developed the pictures together. I loved them so much, and I learned from them what a real family should be like. In fact, I copied their ways in many ways through my life with kids.

I was unable to sleep one early morning and went into the kitchen for a cup of coffee. I could see a rainbow out of my kitchen window. To me it was incredible. I could see the end, and I thought it was so cool. I even checked for a pot of gold at the end, but there was none. I was so excited by its beauty that I called George to tell him about it. I wish I had taken a picture, but I had no camera. I fell back asleep while staring at it. When I got up for the day, it was gone.

Then other friends I made at the Southern Baptist Church tried to get me to rectify my divorce status. My Sunday school class told me that I could never remarry and they encouraged me to do all I could to reunite with Dwayne. It was a long, arduous journey that started by contacting him. He agreed I should come to Indiana for a visit, and I did, along with Tonna. I stayed at his brother Ralph's house.

Imagine my surprise to find Dwayne had a girlfriend. I stayed for a miserable week and a half but I saw no reason to reconcile or break up his new relationship. Tonna and I headed home.

My Sunday school class didn't give up. They determined that it would go better on my own turf, so the new plan was for Dwayne to visit me. They wanted to get to know him. Bear in mind, this was after three years apart. To my surprise, he agreed to visit. He showed interest in reconciliation and started seeing Tonna. He stayed with my mother.

He went to a church dinner and they were shocked to realize he was as bad as I said he was, mouth and all. They realized it wasn't in our best interest to get back together after all. I told him. He told me that he and his girlfriend were having a baby. She was due any day.

He had his girlfriend move to Vermont and their baby girl was born soon after. His girlfriend was nothing but mean to Tonna and me. She hated me and Vermont. In a sudden turn of events, we came back into Dwayne's life, and it all was a waste of time for her and all of us. As it turns out, Dwayne was willing to come to Vermont primarily because he was in trouble in Indiana and needed to get away. They went back there as soon as it was safe for him to return.

My friends at the church were convinced the marriage was over but said I would have to remain single. *Easy for them to say*, I thought. *I was bound to that relationship against my will. Did God really end my life over that and make me stay single?* George and Nancy didn't agree and told me to trust in God.

At the library one day a lady came in, sat on my desk, and said, "I pick you." "What do you mean, you 'pick' me?" I responded. She repeated again, "I pick you. Lunch. Noon." And she left. So I asked my boss, Linda, "What do you know about that strange lady?"

My boss said, "Oh, that's Hugette. She's from Sweden. She's harmless and doesn't know anyone. Her husband told her to be careful how she picks her friends. She just wants to make some friends. She speaks very little English.

Go have fun." ("... so by the one man's obedience the many will be made righteous." Romans 5:19)

She took the "picking" of friends part literally! She indeed brought me to her house and was whistling and all excited while she fixed lunch. Her husband made quite a first impression as well. He walked in, an imposing six plus feet tall. Christopher greeted me and then escorted Hugette to a corner of the kitchen that was out of sight and said, "Who is that?"

"But you told me to pick! I picked her at the library!"

He was not happy with her and said, "You can't walk around picking people and bringing them into our home!"

Christopher came out and said, "Hugette doesn't know our language well. She took me literally about how to pick a friend."

I responded, "Well, to her credit, she has been watching me for a while." "I'm so sorry," he said.

I assured him it was okay. "I thought it was flattering and funny. I've never been picked before. So, what's for lunch?!"

He laughed, turned to her, and said, "I think you did a good job of picking her, Hugette. This is a good one. I like her so we'll keep her. She's now our friend!" We all laughed and had a nice lunch. She made her own bread and it was delicious, out of this world.

We spent a lot of time together. I often read Bible stories to their little girl, Katland, when I baby-sat for them. The little girl, and Christopher too, loved the stories. When Christopher and Hugette arrived home after a night out, they would listen while I finished the stories. Sometimes he invited me to read to them even if they weren't going anywhere. But Hugette hated it! She said God was evil, fire and brimstone. Her background involved mainly negative things she learned about God in Sweden. When she returned from sitting in the cold car where she often retreated with her blanket to avoid listening to the stories, she complained about what I was doing so I'd stop. I assured her I didn't want to upset her. But Chris would say, "We enjoy them. I'm the head of this house, so she can read. If you don't want to listen, you don't have to. And, by the way, you're the one who picked her!" Silence followed. ("For sin will have no dominion over you, since you are not under the law but under grace." Romans 6:14)

That always stopped her complaints for the time being. It wasn't funny at the time, but we look back on it and laugh. And, wouldn't you know, down the road, years later, she started going to the Advent Christian Church. She's still going to that church. By then the church had changed pastors. She and Chris both love the Lord. I wish I could say all of their kids felt the same.

Their son, Brendan, did show an interest in the gospel message at one time. Tragically, he shot himself by accident cleaning his hunting rifle. We were all devastated. The loss was so sad. It took years to adjust to losing him. Chris, Hugette and I have remained friends over the years and the varied distances between us. Their kids are grown and I don't see them often, but we tried for years to get together once a year. They turned out to be one of the nicest couples I ever met; they were like a brother and sister to me. I absolutely love them both and their kids. I miss them.

[**Author's note:** *It's obvious to me now that God was turning me into a different person. I saw things differently. I studied my Bible more. I learned to pray in a more personal way. I saw Him working in my life in different ways. My desires were different. He used me to bring His children to Him, and I obeyed.*]

Chapter 21

Mentors

It is sometimes difficult to recall, or perhaps acknowledge, the parts of my life where I knew I was on the wrong path. It's called not listening to the Lord. My life was a developing experience of growing in faith and what it all meant. During the times I had when I was partying with the girls and drinking, I developed another horrible habit that became an obsession of sorts for a long time, and was eating at me. With some outside influence, I learned to be an expert shoplifter. We spent a good deal of time taking things at random that didn't belong to us. It developed to the point where I outfitted Tonna in the finest clothing, provided delicious food for our table, including steak on occasion, and took a host of other items that caught my fancy. The habit became something I felt I couldn't control for the longest time. I was a self-made kleptomaniac.

After several months of this guilt about what I had done, I decided I had to make amends so I wouldn't worry about going into stores I had been avoiding, even though I loved shopping. I was never proud of what I was doing and I'm mortified thinking back on those days. One day I was in Furman's Store owned by Robert Furman in Springfield. I loved that shop because of the quality of the items he sold, including children's clothing. I realized that day that I'd had enough. God convicted me. He told me in that still, small voice to go to confess to the owner. So I did just that. I said, "I am trying to stop stealing things. I need you to watch me and make sure that I don't take anything that I haven't paid for."

He indeed told his clerks to keep an eye on me, and they did for the next few months whenever I was in the store. One day, Mr. Furman surprised the daylights out of me. He said, "No one is going to watch you anymore.

Not in the fire

You won't take anything from me; I know you won't." I was stunned and said, "Thank you."

He continued, "In fact, I'm going to give you credit. You now have fifty dollars in credit here. Buy whatever you want. When you pay it off, you'll get fifty dollars more in credit."

I was blown away. "Really? You're going to do that for me? I've never had credit in my whole life!"

His reply was the beginning of one of the most important life lessons I have learned. He said, "The proper use of credit is one of the most important concepts you will learn in life, young lady. You've had a rough start, and I'm telling you that if you build your credit, your credit defines your name, your worth, and your trust; you will go far."

That meant so much to me. It was my first line of credit, and it changed me. From then on, if I borrowed and said I would pay someone back, I paid them back. To this day, I have credit in different stores. There are certain stores where I honestly say, "I can't pay you right now. May I pay you next week?" And I'm allowed to take what I need because I've built up that trust, and my word and my name mean something. I always pay my bills.

I "credit" God with helping me to straighten out my life, along with George and Nancy. I was at ease when I was with them, and their kids were close to me as well. Other mentors in my life, such as Claudia and Ronnie, Hugette and Chris, and folks from both churches, not only befriended me, but also provided guidance and support through the years. We are still in touch, even though Claudia is struggling with health issues. Ronnie has always been a source of support to me and he is a great husband to Claudia. Chris, though he twice has confronted cancer, remains a strength in my life. He also is an example of a loving husband and father. I always feel at home with them. Hugette and I share the same birthday among all of the other meaningful connections we have shared over the years. She is like a sister to me. Her kids have been special to me. I so value all of these friendships. I wish I could have found that one person I could love and would love me, but it just has not happened. God has been enough!

I had another interesting experience while I worked at the library. I heard about the daughter of a friend who was in a coma following a car accident. It was a foregone conclusion that she would not survive. The Lord put it on my heart to go to the hospital and pray over her. I wasn't family and she was in intensive care. *What do I do?* I asked that still, small voice that was always with me. "Just walk in. Talk to no one." So I walked right in, past the desk, a nurse, and a doctor. I went up to her, put my mouth next to her ear, and I prayed, "In Jesus' name, you are going to live! You are going to be fine. Trust the Lord. When you wake up, you will seek Jesus and live a better life."

The nurse came in to take her vitals and never saw me; I just moved aside. After the nurse left, I prayed again and then I left. To this day, that girl thinks an angel came to her and said those things. She did find Jesus and lives a better life. God can use us like angels. I feel blessed to be used and have done many things for Christ in my life. I have learned to listen to the voice when I'm told to help others and have responded in a variety of ways. It might entail cleaning someone's house, helping to organize their belongings, fixing up a residence for someone to occupy, or whatever. It is my way of serving the Lord. If anyone asks why I'm doing these things, I respond, "Jesus asked me to help. God says we are to help one another." They seldom reply back. When things did not go well, it was because I went ahead on my own.

I don't ever blame God and I get so upset with myself when I don't do what He says. I was still growing and learning what being a Christian meant. Do we ever stop learning? I do not believe so. It is a lifetime task.

[**Author's note:** *During this part of my life, God used me differently than in the past. I went to hospitals to pray for others and I stepped in to help as I sensed an individual's need. I made friends of all ages, which in turn opened the door for people to see how I had changed. They, in turn, wanted what I had -- God. My family called me a Jesus freak. Oh well, I am!*]

Chapter 22

✦━┄┄┄╌❦❦╌┄┄┄━✦

The Man of My Dreams

Eventually, I was introduced to the cousin of a friend. He was on a visit from South Carolina, where he was the choir director for a huge Southern Baptist Church. John was twenty-four, about four years older than I was at the time. He was not dating anyone; he had just gotten out of college. He was such a gentleman, and it did not bother him that I had a daughter. In fact, he said he admired me for keeping Tonna.

I liked John almost at once. We connected. He was a very nice person and he was good to me. We started dating. He stayed in Vermont for three weeks and he called daily when he returned to South Carolina. We wrote to each other, as well. Eventually, he asked if I could get someone to watch Tonna so that I could meet his mother. He promised to pay for the ticket.

I agreed and took a bus to South Carolina. It sounds crazy, but though we slept in the same bed in his apartment, he never approached me for sex. After my experiences with men, it amazed me. We just cuddled up close, but he wasn't going to ask for anything more until we were married. That was incredible because I had never met a guy like that. He showed me the area, including the ocean, and we had so much fun. I thought I had finally found everything I needed and wanted in a man. He was a Christian, he was kind to me, he had a respectable position in the church, and he wanted me to move down there and marry him! I said I would.

But first I had to meet his mother. We drove to where she lived in North Carolina, and I found out she wasn't happy about meeting me. She heard rumors from her relatives in Vermont about me and Tonna, and she didn't need or want to know anything else. I tried to win her over, but it seemed she could only view me as a hussy after her son. I was so very hurt.

I had a child and wasn't married, and that was all she needed to know. She had no desire to hear any of the explanations I wanted to provide, nor her son's pleas to give me a chance.

When his mother saw him give me a quick hug and kiss while in her backyard, she threw a fit. "You little hussy! Making love to my son right in my own backyard!"

He yelled back, "Mom, I am the one holding her! And we're not making love. Really Mom, you need to stop being mean. We're not doing anything wrong."

She slammed the door when she went back into the house. I had no desire to share a meal with her or stay in her house. I wanted to leave but I couldn't bring myself to tell John. When it was time to go to bed, she slept in the bed with me! She looked at me and said, "I'm sleeping right here. I'm not going to let you get into my son's bed."

He came to the door to say goodnight and he saw her and said, "Mom, this is crazy. Barb is not like that. Why are you doing this?" He left the door open and went to bed after telling me he was so sorry. Neither of us slept that night. I cried silently most of the night. I prayed, *Why, Lord, why? Please help us!*

He drove me back to Springfield with his mother in the front seat. We dropped her off at her brother's house. He then drove me home and we went inside. He held me, kissed me good-bye, and said, "I am so sorry. This could have been the best thing ever to happen to me. I really do love you, and I care for your daughter. I thought I finally had the right person in my life, but I just can't go against my mother. I'm her only child, and she'll be able to make our lives miserable. She'll never accept you, ever, not until she dies. As ornery as she is, she'll live forever."

I was heartbroken. I did nothing but cry for three months. I didn't want to eat; I didn't care about anything. I lost a lot of weight. I just didn't understand. That "still, small voice" said we cannot change sinful actions of others, and there are no choices to inflict their un-Godly behavior onto others. He walked away and never talked to me again. I have no idea what happened to him. For a long time, I was so devastated I hardly talked to anyone. It was so hard. Tonna and I just got on with our lives and my job at the library. *Will the right one ever come?* I lost weight; my friends, my pastor and my mother were concerned.

George was there every night to talk with me on the phone so I could sleep. He'd say prayers with his family with me on the phone. They'd

Not in the fire

all say, "Good night, Aunt Barb," and go to bed. Then he and Nancy would share so many Bible stories with me until I fell asleep. It was so nice. I love them so. They're both in heaven now.

Chapter 23

Is This the One?

After a few months of losing weight and staying away from everyone, Lila, the same girlfriend who introduced me to John, called and asked if I would go with her to her mom's funeral. I said yes. I loved her mom and was sad to hear she had died of cancer.

At the funeral, I shook hands with Lila's stepfather, Raymond, and told him how sorry I was for his loss. After the funeral, I returned home and struggled to resume a more normal existence. Lila told me how deeply sorry she was about John and that her aunt was hard to live with and always had been. She tried to reassure me that time would heal my heart. I still worked at the library at that time.

About ten months after the funeral, Lila called to ask another favor. She asked If I would go out to supper with her stepfather. She wanted to get him out of the house and perhaps stop brooding over his loss of her mom. He was very nice and so lonely, and so was I.

I agreed. I needed to get out, even if just to have a nice dinner and to dance a little. To my surprise, we connected in a way I did not expect. We talked until the place closed. When he touched me, I felt weak in the knees and got goose bumps all over. It was like with John. Was God opening a new door? No mother to interfere anyway!

We started dating. We had fun snowmobiling. We hiked, canoed, fished and went on motorcycle rides. We went to My Lady Bike Blessing in Colebrook, NH. I still have the ribbon. He had kids who got along well with Tonna. His son, David, and I went bottle digging. He was a wonderful kid and we became close.

I helped David get a job with me doing dishes at the senior center, where I worked on weekends, a second job for me. We worked well together. His sister Donna and I had long talks about girl things; we were a good fit as well. Many in his family went to church, so I started going with them to the Faith Baptist Church, Pastor Laveen. After a year and a half of dating, Raymond took me to the Hungry Lion steak house and proposed, offering me a beautiful ring. I still have the box with the date on it. We decided to get married as soon as we could. I loved his family. He had lots of sisters and they all liked me. One was into Mary Kay™ Cosmetics and we traveled all over. We announced we were engaged and everyone at church was happy for us. All around us people supported our being together. I was incredibly happy!

Then I moved in with him. I know I should have waited until we were married, but the move was prompted by Lila's and her sister's decision to strip his mobile home of everything their mother had purchased. Raymond was at work at the time and they left the mobile home just about empty. We were getting married, I had a lot of stuff that we just were going to have to get rid of anyway, and it was nicer than what the daughters had taken. We thought my moving in made sense.

We were settled in when Lila's sister, who was a bully and also the wife of a gang member, came to the mobile home. She was furious and exclaimed that she was not going to let me live in her mother's home. ("Let the lying lips be mute." Psalms 31:18a)

All I could think was, not again! We both were devastated and couldn't understand her attitude. It was his home now. Her mother had been gone for nearly three years, and he began arguing with her, pointing out she had taken all of her mother's stuff without asking. He reminded her that he let her get away with it and never said a word.

I turned to retreat to the bathroom but she followed me in and slammed the door behind us. She yelled at me for being there and pushed me into the sink. I told her I was not going to fight with her. So she slapped my face and mocked, "You Christians are supposed to turn the other cheek!" I did and she repeatedly slapped my face. I refused to hit her back. I felt sorry for her since she was grieving her mother's death and she also had just found out she had cancer. I did try to reason with her and said, "I don't see what the problem is here."

She blurted, "Yeah well it just is! You're one of those goodie two-shoes Christians. I don't see God helping you now!" I said, "God is my avenger and He will do what He sees fit to do. I'm not to take things into my own hands. I will not hit you!"

She kept slapping my face until I was numb. Raymond was trying to bust in when she opened the door and flew out. I heard her screaming in the kitchen. I'm not sure why I pursued her, but I did. She grabbed me by my hair and slammed my head into the cupboard. Raymond pulled her off and kicked her out the door. He was so worried about me he took me to the hospital. The hospital called the police; I was a mess. They asked me what happened, wrote up a report and pressed charges. She ended up in jail for thirty days and the court put a restraining order on her and she got a hefty fine, since I lived there. When she was released she was not allowed to go within a mile of me.

After my release from the hospital, Raymond thought it best for me to go to my mother's. I just laid on the couch and cried. I wondered what would happen. Tonna was worried about me. Finally, Raymond called and said he missed me and wanted me to come home. We resumed plans to be married. The daughter called Henry at work shortly after and said that if he married me, she would show up at the wedding and blow my head off.

Raymond took what she said seriously. I awoke the next morning to find a check for a thousand dollars, accompanied by a note asking me to leave. He said he believed she would do what she said and he couldn't bury another wife. He said he loved me enough to let me go. Why not love me enough to press charges?

Nearly everything in the house was mine, but I couldn't strip the house clean. He had two dependent children, Donna and David, whom I loved. So I took Tonna, our personal belongings, and the check, and I left.

Tonna and I went directly to New Hampshire where I left her with my brother Keith. I kissed her goodbye and said, "I'm sorry. I'm going away, and you're going to live with Uncle Keith." I left him the check in an envelope to help with her care.

I drove to a remote area of town, parked in the bushes at an abandoned gas station, and took an overdose of pills, hoping it would be over soon and telling myself, *I can't do this anymore; I am never going to make it in this world.* There was no more use trying. I just wanted to be with my Father in heaven. He loved me as I was. Tonna would be better off with anyone but me.

I knew my time was short. I felt tired. I had the sudden urge to call my dad and say goodbye. I got out of the car walked to the pay phone booth just a short walk away. When Dad answered, all I could say was, "I am sorry. I can't do this. Life is too hard and painful." That's all I could say. I dropped the phone and stumbled back to the car before I passed out. (Note: The phone cord was cut and it was no longer in service, I was told later.)

My dad was devastated but he acted quickly. He called the police and suicide hot line. They traced the call and were able to find me. I was still passed out. They said it was about thirty minutes later when the police and ambulance arrived. They were not able to wake me up so they got me into the ambulance. On the way to hospital I woke up a little and then I passed out again. My mother was at the hospital by the time I arrived. I was close to death. They told her they were not sure they could save me. They started CPR when my heart stopped and gave me shots. I surfaced to hear my mother yelling. She was pounding on me and saying, "You're not going to die!" I drifted in and out of full awareness of what was happening and I remember watching for a minute before I started to go up toward a great light. *I would soon see Jesus.*

I remember thinking, *Yay, Lord, I can finally leave this life.* But as I got closer, the Lord said, Your time is not yet. You have much to do. You need to go back. I said, *Please I don't want to go back there*, but then all of a sudden I was back in my body, and my mother was crying and yelling, "You're not going to die!" I groaned and thought, do I really have to come back to this? They were able to wake me up again, and they gave me a sickening substance to make me throw up. It was awful.

Eventually, they put me in the suicide ward. All told, I was hospitalized for two weeks. Raymond got the car and never came to see me; he thought it was best. It was so boring, and I didn't want to be there. The high point was when my father came to see me and said, "Barbara Jean, I'm bringing you home with me. You need a new start."

I was discharged and went home with him. I never wanted to go back to Springfield again, ever! It was bad luck. Nothing went right for me there. For the time being, I wanted nothing to do with anyone in Springfield, not even the Southern Baptist nor the Advent Christian churches. I was just too embarrassed to have messed up again. The only folks from there who mattered were Claudia, Ronnie, Chris and Hugette, and George and Nancy! I was done with everyone else and wanted to start over. We kept in touch by telephone, but I didn't want to go to Springfield.

My grandparents were part of my life and they were sad for what I had been through. Raymond and the kids struggled with my absence and their lives were a mess, as well. We all were hurting because of one pathetic person's jealousy and refusal to move on. I wondered how one person could dictate what a stepfather could do with his life. I did not hate God. It was her sin I battled with, not God. I was mad at myself for not moving in. No matter what, I should have waited. God may have had Raymond move out, sell the mobile home, get his own place for us. Who knows? I just messed it up again. (The crazy thing is, I repeat the same ordeal in the future! When will I learn?) Thus, I remained confused and despondent. I was prescribed medicine but it was a church in Brattleboro that helped me rebuild my life.

[**Author's note**: *This chapter of my life was very, very painful. I loved Raymond and the kids. I had lost them and nearly all I owned. I struggled with God about why this was happening. But I remembered that Jesus said to me that my work was not done. So I would live for Him. I was not sure how, but I would find out as I went along. And I was my own worst enemy.*]

Chapter 24

A New Life with Dad

On my way to Dad's house in Brattleboro upon my release, we stopped by my mother's place in Springfield to pick up Tonna. Much to my disappointment, Keith's wife had refused to keep her. I didn't want her at Mom's but he had no choice. I cried and prayed myself to sleep every night for a long time.

Tonna and I had an apartment in the back upper level of my dad's house. He was frightened for me and told me he never wanted me to try to take my own my life again. He said he had lived without me all of those years and he couldn't bear it if I died. He was very emotional as he told me I was his firstborn child that lived and he would die inside if anything happened to me. So I settled in. Dad and I grew close once again. I wanted to regularly attend the church I had located, but Raymond took back the car we had bought together and I couldn't afford another one. People were giving me so many nice things to fill my apartment. I didn't need a car as yet. God was still taking care of me. His still, small voice was trying to get through to me, but I shut it out much of the time. I was still so hurt I just gave Him my tears. My pain ached; it was hard to hear Him through it.

Raymond surprised me with a visit and spent the night. He held me all night. We both cried. He was sad that Tonna and I were so far away, but he knew it was better to be away from his step-children. Donna and David missed me. He also missed me yet had no idea how we could make it work. I was hopeful we still had a chance.

Raymond brought all of my personal stuff in boxes my mom had packed up. I was not happy she was in my stuff at all and she took it upon herself to burn all of the memories of everyone that had been in my life before. I never got over that. What right did she have to do that?

He took me with him to his pastor, Pastor Laveen, for counseling the next day. The pastor told me we never should have moved in together, though he was so sorry for his step-children's actions. He said he didn't see us being together unless Raymond was willing to confront the issues and put them in their place. I attempted to explain to the pastor how much we had missed each other and what had transpired between us, which was that Raymond came, spent the night, and told me that he loved me. I thought this session was about how we could proceed with our relationship.

Instead, the pastor said hardly anything, mostly negative things addressed to Raymond. He turned to me and said if I needed him at all to call him, but Raymond needed to deal with the situation. It was his place to fix this mess. Raymond said nothing.

My mother came and took me home to Brattleboro. I was upset all over again. I got counseling, lost my job, and went on welfare. I refused to leave my apartment and went back to crying all the time. I seldom ate and became weak. Poor Tonna was alone through all this. Then I developed bronchitis. ("A joyful heart is good medicine, but a crushed spirit dries up the bones." Proverbs 17:22)

Dad knew how much trouble I was in with my health. He came to my apartment and put his foot down, saying, "Enough, young lady, you have a daughter. You're not in this alone. Get up and move on. Get a job. You know you can do it, you have before."

So I got a job in the meat department of the local Price Chopper. I liked the job. I worked with men for the most part. They were funny and joked a lot, yet respectful to me. One day, they told me I needed to prepare an order of chicken lips. I was dumb-founded, but they were serious. So I went in the cooler to find some chicken lips. I finally came out of the cooler and said, "Where are they?" They all bent over laughing. I had suspected it was a joke, but I wasn't sure because they sold some weird meat in that place. I could have wrung their necks.

They continued to needle me about it. That wasn't enough. It seemed that everyone in the store heard about it. Even customers would come to the window and ask me for chicken lips. It never got old for them. It always set off a round of laughter. It took a while, but I laughed also.

Not in the fire

I followed that job with a motel next door as a chambermaid. Then I became a dietary aide filling meal orders for patients. I visited the patients to see what they wanted for the week's meals; I loved to see the residents. That led to being offered a dishwasher's job at the Advent Christian home and I grabbed it. It paid more money. I worked with an African American man who was very nice. I met his family and we became friends. I found I was not nervous about our friendship, despite the horror I had witnessed when that young couple was burned for their interracial relationship.

I took a cab to and from work and got to know the cab owner. He was an older man who gave me a break on fees. Gary, my cousin, also worked for the cab owner and would pick me up after Tonna was in bed some evenings. I'd sit in the front and ride in the cab with him and his fares. We had a lot of laughs as we rode around for hours.

I had hardly seen my half- and step-brothers and sisters for years, but we became reacquainted while I stayed in the apartment over my dad. I made sure they got to know Tonna, but the visits were infrequent, and we had a lot of catching up to do. Sally was good to me. She loved Tonna. Until she became ill, she helped to take care of Tonna after school.

Sally had very little time from finding out she had cancer until her death. She was in a nursing home in her final days and wanted to say goodbye to Tonna. Tonna sat in her lap and talked to her. She also sang, Jesus Loves Me to her. Sally told Dad to take us out for supper and get Tonna an ice-cream from her. So we assumed she needed to sleep. That night she passed on.

The funeral was so difficult for all of us, especially her kids. ("For here we do not have an enduring city, but we are looking for the city that is to come." Hebrews 13:14) It was good to see Tommy. He was married and happy. Both he and his wife were in the Air Force and worked as air traffic controllers. Brenda was there and had taken time off from flight attendant training. Two of the kids were still in high school and junior high school; Billy was only nine years old. Dad was devastated. He was devoted to Sally. I told him I was there and would help.

After work one evening, he wanted to go out to just be alone. He went to the pub but he promised he would not get drunk. I stayed and watched the kids. It became late and I could not figure out what happened. I was just about to go look for him when he walked in with a nurse who had treated Sally. They both were drunk. They had struck up a deal that they would get married. She would take care of him, the house, and the kids in exchange for a place to live. She had squandered her money and was being evicted from her apartment. Her kids were grown and lived on their own. She was a drunk and smoked a lot.

So they arrived and proceeded to go to bed. I was shocked and worried about the kids' reaction in the morning since the arrangement certainly didn't set well with me. He said he did not want me to feel it was my job to care for all of them since my mother had done that to me all my life.

This woman seemed mean and I did not like her. She was harsh with Tonna and she never wanted us to hang around with the kids. The kids would spend a lot of time upstairs with me. I had a talk with Dad, who was upset and had a long talk with her. She made some changes, but I could tell she hated me. She wanted no young kids around.

A new owner at the Advent Christian home replaced all of the staff, so I looked for a different job, yet visited all the residents. I had dated my dentist a couple of times, but that did not work out. He wasn't looking for a serious relationship, and I was. Then I started a Girl Scout troop for Tonna and I moved into the bigger front apartment in the same building. I liked that place and was still near Dad. I was still hurting inside and confused as to what God wanted from me. I continued to go to church and read devotionals.

One day, an old friend named Mickey came for a visit. I had, long before, jumped on the back of his bike and he became my mechanic/friend. He was the one who talked me through the acid trip. He said he had loved me for years. He told me he was finally leaving his wife, who would not give up illicit drugs. His kids were grown and independent. So he wanted me to marry him and move out west to start over.

I was flattered. I went over in my head that no one had ever loved me that long hoping to be with me. We had never been more than best friends. He had been good to me. He fixed my car and was the one who read *Alice in Wonderland* to me. He would have a "talk" with any guy that took advantage of me.

Back then, he was married and off limits. For years he was in the background. On occasion he would call or stop by for coffee and to see how I was, but never tried to do anything except to be a friend. He gave me a kiss and said, "I can't call or see you until my divorce is over." He left.

I'm not sure why, but I didn't believe him. It was just another let down and I wasn't going to go there again. *Why would he really want me?* Besides, I didn't want to move out west. I never looked at him as a boyfriend, though he was a good catch. He didn't believe in God, though, and I knew I couldn't

Not in the fire

date anyone who was not saved. And mostly God said, "NO!"

Many times, over the years when I was alone and wondered how I would pay the rent or even put food on the table, my needs were met in nothing short of miraculous ways. I never had to worry. Instead, I prayed, *I've asked you, Lord. I know you'll take care of us. What do you want from me Lord?* ("For I know the plans I have for you, declares the Lord, plans for welfare and not for evil, to give you a future and hope." Jeremiah 29:11)

I started going to a new church, yet I was leery about getting close to anyone and hadn't got close to anyone yet. I didn't know any one well enough to ask for help. Yet no one would come get us on Sunday and it was too far to walk for Tonna. So we stopped going. I was still visiting the Advent Home and loved the old people there. The ladies were so sweet to me. I never asked them for anything, though many were wealthy. I just liked them, and they loved Tonna. I still had no car and I took a cab to and from work every day. I noticed an ad in the paper for a class on modeling in Brattleboro. I wanted to do this for so long, but it cost a thousand dollars. I called Raymond and asked if he could please help me to go. He sent me a check for one thousand dollars and I used it to sign up for Barbizon modeling school and to help me with living expenses for a time.

He told me he was blown away that his kids loved me so much and had wanted to come and live with me for a long time, but he always said no. At this point, neither of the kids were doing well. Yet, despite their fond memories of me, they did not attempt to visit me over the years. Eventually, David went into the service to get away and Donna simply remained a mess. I loved them both, but I never saw them again.

My dad was supportive of my work with Barbizon. He thought it would build my self-image and it did. I enjoyed it. It was an eight-week course. Tonna stayed with my younger sister Kendra. I still had the photos from George and I had a photographer ask to take photos of me by the river for a magazine. I loved going to school evenings. When I graduated, I had a big ceremony and was so glad my mom and Grandma Grover came to watch. We went out to eat afterwards; Gram was so proud of me.

By this time I was about twenty-one and I got a job working for Barbizon modeling school in Hartford, CT. My sister Kendra came back and lived with me to watch Tonna for a few months in the summer so I could go. They wanted me to get girls to sign up for modeling and supervise the bus down to a class in Hartford once a week. I got my photo in the newspapers in Brattleboro and in Springfield, as well. The girls I recruited were would-be models for two, eight-week classes and I loved it but not enough of them signed up for a third course so I lost that job.

I was offered a job modeling in Connecticut, but I hated cities the size of Hartford and had no intention of raising my daughter there. So I did not pursue it.

I got another job at the mall in a store that sold baby clothes. They had seen my photo in the paper. I was doing well, setting up displays and stocking supplies. After almost two years, they had to downsize when things became slow. Since I was new, I was the first to go. Luckily, the manager of a sportwear store (Jaymar Ruby) across the hall hired me to work as a junior manager. I loved it. I even catered my boss' wedding for her.

[**Author's note:** *At this point I had been wounded so badly. I felt so alone and confused and wondered what was next. I wallowed in my misery for a period of time. But I got up, and God helped me to start over. I learned to depend on Jesus daily, and things started moving forward.*]

Chapter 25

A New Development

Tonna was in sixth grade by this time and she roused the interest of an individual in the neighborhood who noticed her at the kitchen window of the young gentleman next door. He was a policeman, and a really handsome one. I heard her talking to him one day and I asked him if she was bothering him. He said, "T.J.? No way. She is a sweet girl." That's where she got the nickname, T.J.

I said, "Thank you," and their quick conversations went on for a while. Every day she knew when he would leave for work, arrive home for lunch, and return home in afternoon. They laughed and talked.

He had a very cool, yellow Camaro. She asked one day if she could have a ride and he said, "Maybe someday." He seemed to really like Tonna and acted as though he was looking forward to meeting her every day. If she missed a day, he'd yell up at me if he saw me in front of the window doing dishes and ask, "Is T.J. ok?" *Strange how we're getting connected because of a young girl.* I never would have dared to try to date a police officer on my own.

One day I called the police station to see if my six Girl Scouts could visit the jail on a field trip. They agreed and said they would send someone over to pick us up. The desk sergeant set up a time and date then said, "I know just the tour guide for you! Where should he pick up the troop?" I gave him my address, which is where the troop met. Little did I know that Thomas talked about Tonna with the guys at work.

It was Thomas, Tonna's friend, who showed up in a police van to take us to the police station. I recognized him right away as the officer out the window.

I was a little embarrassed, knowing my daughter liked him so much.

She, of course, was tickled to death it was Thomas. He made a "Three Stooges" face and a noise that she loved, which made all the girls laugh.

It was a snowy winter and Thomas managed to drive the van into a snowbank at the station. He said, "That's ok, I'll help you all out." One at a time he lifted the girls out of the van. Other officers were watching and cheering him on. Then he came to get me. I was blushing but he just smiled and winked. He was nervous too, I could tell. He lifted me out like I weighed nothing. He was so cute; this was the closest I had gotten to him so far. While we had our tour, the other officers got the van out of the snowbank. Thomas took us home.

He had my phone number from the office call list, so two days later he called and asked if I would go to a police Christmas party banquet. I said I would like that. Thus, we started dating. My dad loved him and so did Tonna. Dad invited us to supper several times.

I soon met Thomas' family, as well, and we all got along, though his parents were hesitant at first because I was older by five years and had a child. But they loved Tonna and could see how much Thomas loved her.

Soon, we fell in love, or so I thought. His first real dating experience was with me and that had me concerned, but everything seemed to be going well. It wasn't long before he asked me to marry him and he gave me a ring.

And it wasn't long after that I received a call from none other than Mickey, telling me his divorce was final and he was free. He was looking forward to us starting over and wanted to come to Brattleboro. I was stunned. I explained that after a year with no word from him, I had moved on. I explained to him that I was engaged to a terrific police officer, had grown close to my fiancé's family, and I had no intention of ending the relationship.

Mickey asked if I loved him. I said I cared for him a lot, but I emphasized that I was happy, that love is a choice. I had learned the hard way. I explained that I no longer believed love was emotional or romantic. I was learning to be realistic, and I chose to love Thomas. I had been hurt so many times in my life that I wasn't letting my heart go there. I told Mickey that I was not sure I knew what love was any longer. It was enough for me that Tonna loved him.

He said to me, "Well, I know I love you. Please don't do this!" When he knew I wasn't going to change my mind then and there, he insisted that I call him if I changed my mind. He added, "I'll respect your choice," and we said goodbye.

I cried, I was confused, but I was determined that God was in my plans to marry Thomas. My whole family was behind me. My sisters were planning to be in the wedding. So was George's son, Nathan. Everything had fallen together so well.

We had a beautiful wedding at the Baptist Church in Brattleboro. It was a dream wedding. Mom and I catered it all for two hundred or more people. His parents had a big rehearsal dinner with all their friends, family and my parents at a grand hotel. "The works," one might say. It was so nice. As a wedding gift, the cab driver who took me to work drove a shuttle for the nursing home residents to the wedding. They filled the first three rows. It was wonderful to see them all dressed up.

This was in April of 1983. We also planned a wonderful honeymoon trip to the Pocono mountains and we visited the Pennsylvania Amish country. But Thomas wasn't all that romantic at first. He wanted to watch the Bruins. It became apparent that he was afraid of intimacy. I took a bubble bath and went for a walk, watching all the other couples in love. I was so envious, but we were married; somehow it was going to be okay.

We settled into a routine at home. Thomas was raised in the church, but there were no signs that he practiced his faith. I sensed he was what we had always referred to as a "backslidden" Christian. ("Let not sin therefore reign in your mortal body, to make you obey its passions." Romans 6:12) I adored Thomas' physique and thought how lucky I was to have him! I still wasn't looking at the inside since I was still hurting from Raymond. Once we were married, I saw a bit more about what was going on inside of him and became unsure about the marriage, sadly, but I was determined to give it my best. Still, he showed few signs of intimacy. I wanted more.

Thomas was a good father to Tonna, and he even adopted her emotionally and legally. We had plans for more children. After all of the prayers and medical tests, Thomas became very depressed. Though we followed all recommendations, we were never able to conceive. We found out that Thomas was not able to have children.

I assured him it was okay but he knew I wanted more kids. I trusted God for His best, but it ate away at Thomas. He started pulling away from me in more ways than one. He worked more. I was scared. To add to the strain, my family started to bring their problems to me. Some of the problems were significant and Thomas did not know how to deal with them.

I was so stressed out with my mom at one point that I threw a bowl of food at her and told her to just leave. At the time, we were still trying to conceive and I explained that to Mom. The family was stressing Thomas and me to the limit. She left and we did not talk for several weeks.

My sister was pregnant and abandoned at a hotel by her ex-husband. She had the baby alone and was sick. The hotel owner called me for help and I had to respond. I withdrew money from our savings and sent my mom and Kenny to get her. Thomas tried to understand, but the situation took its toll. Our savings was supposed to help us get our own place.

I felt guilty because I was responsible for introducing my sister to the man who abandoned her. What had happened was that soon after I got out of the hospital I visited with Chris and Hugette since I was in Springfield. A male acquaintance of theirs arrived while I was at their house. He wasn't attractive but he seemed nice. I wasn't looking for anyone in my life because I was still in love with Raymond, but when he offered me a ride back to my mother's house to pick up Tonna, I accepted. It seemed convenient at the time. Then he offered to take me and Tonna home to Brattleboro, as he was going that way. My mother was happy for the offer since she was low on gasoline and money.

I didn't realize until later what a mistake this was. He had emotional issues and now he knew where I lived. He called often and I kept putting him off. Dad suggested there would be no harm in having a supportive friend.

Dad's suggestion made sense, so I agreed when this man, Bob, asked if we would go to New York with him to help at his parents' house. He promised Tonna and me privacy in our own room at their home. He seemed to accept the fact that I just wanted to be friends until the night before we left New York. He came to the room where we were staying, got on his knees and asked if I would marry him. It was unbelievable, and I told him no, of course. I explained again that we were just friends.

He was quiet all the way home and I stopped hearing from him for a short time, but I did receive a call from my mother informing me that he was dating my sister. He took her to her prom in a limo and he made it quite the event. My sister was smitten with him. I made no pretense that I was not in favor of the relationship and simply told Mom, "No!"

Mom asked if something had happened, and I told her. In turn, she tried to warn my sister, who wouldn't listen. She instead contended that I was jealous because he dumped me. Of course, he asked her to marry him. And she did, in Mom's back yard. It was a small wedding.

Before the wedding, his parents and I tried to convince him to give the relationship some time.

So they married. I arrived home from the wedding later in the evening and around 11:00 p.m. Dad called and said Bob was outside my home. *What was he doing here? Wasn't he on his honeymoon?* Sure enough, there he was. I opened my door and he came in. He said we had to talk and that my sister was at a hotel in town waiting for him.

He said, "If you promise that you will marry me, I'll annul this wedding and take her home. I don't love her. If you say no again, I will take her, use her and you'll never see her again." I stared at him in disbelief. "Are you out of your mind? She loves you! I could never hurt her like that. Please don't do this."

He left incredibly angry. I couldn't tell anyone because I didn't think they would believe me. Yet Tonna was in her room and heard the whole conversation. She was worried for her Auntie Kendra. I got on my knees and we prayed and trusted her to God. We didn't see or hear from her until the hotel called after she gave birth to Kathleen. I had to help her.

To add to the strain, I received a call from George. He was dying of cancer. He asked what was going on and I told him. He wanted to give me the money to replace my savings in the hope I could heal that particular blow to my marriage. He wanted my marriage to work. I told him he had kids, his wife, and now his health to worry about. I assured him I would be fine. I knew God would help us.

Thomas was supportive of my visiting George and Nancy more often after the onset of George's illness. Nancy took George to a hospital in Pennsylvania for special liver treatments. He died there. His death nearly crushed me. His kids were older now. Nancy remarried after two years. She, too, died of cancer. It's sad that I haven't been in consistent contact with their kids. I miss them but I understand they are married and involved in various ministries.

My brother's first marriage was failing at this time, as well, and Brian stayed with us at various intervals. My mother still depended on me during her many crises and she didn't hesitate to show up unannounced for money or whatever she needed. Thomas was tired of helping them. I was so confused and pulled apart. I had been there all my life for them. *Could I just dump them?*

George was no longer there to mentor me. I just kept praying. We had been attending a church in Charlemont, MA. It was different and Thomas liked it, yet even that didn't seem to help us. There was so much strife between us because of my family. I longed for Thomas to be as supportive as George had been.

By 1987, he decided he no longer wanted to be married to me. He said he was there for T.J., but I needed someone who could give me kids. It was still eating at him he couldn't give me children, even if my family "drove him nuts." Eventually he said that was not the whole reason he didn't want to be married to me. He decided he never had been in love with me. His family tried to talk some sense into him but he still asked me for a divorce. I realized we both had made a mistake and I couldn't be mad at him. We parted friends. Thomas stayed in touch with Tonna for a long time but he faded from that relationship, too. Four years later, he remarried. She didn't want kids and worked at the jail with him. His wife died a few years later of breast cancer shortly after the death of his mother, also of breast cancer.

I had stayed in touch with his mother before her death. We had lunch once a week and talked about the things of the Lord. I was told she was in her chair reading her Bible when she passed, which helped me to feel at peace. I had tried to get her to come to church with us. I missed her. She was a good friend, and she was attentive to Tonna. As a grandmother, in her eyes that wouldn't change.

Not in the fire

Chapter 26

Native American Roots

Though I loved God and His presence in my life was important to me, the time I devoted to Him was slim. I thought I was too busy with my many problems. Looking back, I don't understand why I didn't turn to Him as I had in the past. I was attending church and I started singing in the choir.

I continued my job at a local rest home where I performed a variety of tasks. I loved my bosses. I also did private work for four elderly women, all of whom were wealthy. I cleaned and provided personal care assistance for them. We had nice times as we talked about their past experiences.

I attended Greenfield Community College (GCC) in Massachusetts and did well. I was taking typing, accounting, and English. Tonna was at school while I was at school. I had gotten a newer small car when Thomas and I were married and I kept that car. He kept his yellow Camaro. I missed that car.

I missed Thomas too, far more than I thought I would. I was so hoping he'd come around. Prior to his marriage, I asked him, "Will we ever get back together?" He answered, "I like being alone." Then he repeated, "I don't believe I really loved you. I'm sorry. I hope everything works out for you."

Tonna and I were in a small, one-bedroom apartment. I made the living room my room and we were doing okay. I had always been interested in my Native American ancestry and Tonna and I began attending Native American ceremonies. I met a cousin on my dad's side, Bee, who was a Red Hawk Woman. She took us to Canada, where I met other native people. They made ceremonial regalia for me and Tonna. It was exciting for me and it was good to have weekends where I wasn't sitting at home feeling sorry for myself. I also met Running Deer and joined his medicine society, which taught the use of herbs, natural medicines, and learning to live off the land. I explained I was a Christian and they accepted my prayers to God at meetings.

I played drums, learned to do crafts, and to speak the native language. I received the native name of Evening Star and Tonna was Mother Rabbit. I met other cousins from the Abenaki tribe in Maine and visited there, as well. It was cool hunting moose and everyone was good to us.

As I learned about the policies and broken promises they endured from our government, it broke my heart. I grew closest to Ray and Liz. They had places in Canada and New York. I met their family and found out that they were Seventh Day believers. Over time, I shared with them about my faith in God. In turn, they came to our house. We're still friends today.

I met a host of people representing my Native American heritage. Both of my grandparents were from the Abenaki tribe. I believe the Lord led me to intervene at least a couple of times during my association there.

While attending one of the Native American events, Tonna and I browsed along the crafts and food tables. When we arrived at a particular booth, operated by an older man, we noticed he had a hard time breathing. No one else was around at the time. I asked a few other vendors if they knew him and they said he was George White Bear. That still, small voice told me to offer my help to him, to watch his stand, get food for him, or whatever he needed. Tonna helped also. We loved it. He was so overwhelmed. No one else had offered to help him, so he asked why I did. I told him Jesus loved him and told me to help him.

At the end of the day, he asked us to camp behind his RV and he would offer protection while we camped. We did, and the next day he gave us both dresses to wear while we helped him. He let us keep them. We stayed for the weekend and helped him pack up when it was time to go. He took my address.

He told his family about us and he told all of them about "my Jesus" who tells people to help others. They were far away in Colorado, but they said they wanted to check it out. We had a few visits from them over the years. I'm not sure if they accepted the Lord, but the seeds were planted.

Late in life, Running Deer planned to get married. He asked us to his wedding. We had grown close as family over the years. He surprised me by asking me to pray to my God/Jesus to bless their wedding. I did and I had a lot of people ask questions after the prayer. I got to talk about Jesus and how He asked me to care for others. I was careful to be respectful of their faith and practices but it planted seeds. It was a great day. We danced native dances, which were different yet respectful of women. I learned a lot about their lives and they about mine. I found a lot of native people were so giving and, like me, tried to help others. They said my desire to help was the native blood in me. I knew it was also God.

[**Author's note:** *Life had been full of ups and downs for me and I wasn't sure why I had to go through this again. Should I have tried harder to keep Thomas? I was empty inside. Added to years of pain was another stab in the heart. I wasn't talking to God as often as I should or had in the past. I escaped into my native world. The powwows allowed Tonna and me to travel all over and forget the busy days at work and school. God was still a part of me, but I wondered why nothing ever lasted for me and what I was doing that was so wrong.*]

Chapter 27

A Twentieth Century Betrothal

Thomas no longer went to church after our divorce but I continued to go to the one we had attended together. I met a man named Arthur there. He and his wife had been separated for five years. His wife showed up at church off and on and sat in the same location whenever she attended, the right side in the back of the church, along with whoever was her newest boyfriend.

I wasn't interested in Art. I missed Thomas and still felt the impact of the failed relationship. My goal with regard to important decisions in my life was to simply wait on God! ("…he gave the right to become children of God." John 1:12)

Arthur's situation drew a lot of attention from others, though. His mother sat in front with him and his two kids, or sometimes three kids when the oldest agreed to attend. The kids were so noisy it was hard not to notice them. MJ, the four-year-old, ran in and out all through the service and usually slammed the door each way. Then his daughter AJ chased after MJ. So it went every Sunday. Arthur had no control over the kids' behaviors, and their mother was no help since they ignored what she said. The grandmother seemed to notice but she didn't interfere.

Arthur was into town politics, sang in the choir, and was active in other ways in the church but he seemed lost as to how to deal with his children. I perceived he was doing his best.

Arthur's wife asked Tonna, who was around seventeen, to babysit from time to time. The pastor suggested that she pick me up a few times on Sunday to provide a ride to church for me. She was a strange lady, though very smart. Most of what I knew of Arthur initially was through my involvement in the

Not in the fire

choir and what his children told Tonna. ("My flesh and my heart may fail; but God is the strength of my heart and my portion forever." Psalm 73:26)

Arthur and I became better acquainted during our studies at the local community college. He was studying for his master's degree while I was studying bookkeeping and accounting. I loved it. For once, I was doing well in school!

Every evening, three times a week, Arthur would come to where I had supper and ask to join me. I agreed and he talked away. We would study some and then we would return to our respective classes.

He began to wave when he saw me at church. We received many stares from those around us when I waved back. Then one day at school he asked if I would like to go out for an ice-cream after AJ's volleyball game. I agreed. I enjoyed the game and AJ went home with a friend after we were formally introduced.

MJ drove me nuts during the game, though. He ran continually up the bleachers and under them. He joined us when we went for ice-cream and insisted on a large cone. I thought, *that will make him even more hyper!* And he was. Once again he was under the table, getting into things, and in the way of the waitstaff. Arthur chatted and let him do whatever he wanted. Finally, MJ fell asleep in the seat next to Arthur.

We learned we had a lot in common so he asked me out again on a double date with a couple named Frankie and Bonnie. After all these years, Bonnie and I are still good friends. We had a great time without the kids but I knew if we were going to keep dating, I wanted to get to know the kids. I started having them over on occasion. Tonna knew them, as well, from watching them at their mother's house, so they started to settle down. We grew on each other. In a short amount of time, they learned to do what I asked.

AJ was essentially scared of everything. The oldest, Alan, used to call her BOO. I made him stop by explaining it wasn't helping her. She was afraid of the dark. We would get calls all the time when we went out with friends asking when we were coming home. This happened even when we were at the bottom of the hill eating with friends. She did not get along with her mother at that time and neither did MJ. Alan would do whatever his mother said just to get her attention, but she mostly took the other children for visits and left him home with Art or with his grandmother.

Their mom could not handle all of them at the same time. Alan and I got along, but it was a big adjustment. He was seventeen years old, the same as Tonna. I understood what it must be like for him. He would go to his room and cry. I felt sad for him. He desired his mother's approval even to the point of spying on us for her. It was heartbreaking how she was willing to use her own kids in that way.

Eventually, Arthur asked if I would marry him and I said yes. I cared for him and the kids in the same way he cared for me and Tonna. He admitted he needed someone to take over, get his house in order, and help his kids. He was out of his element and, as they got older, he felt it more. His mom, Betty, also found the kids hard to deal with.

So one day Arthur decided it was time to file for a divorce and that's when his wife stepped up her efforts to interfere. A divorce meant she could no longer show up and sponge money off him whenever she wanted. Art put his foot down; he insisted that after six years of separation she needed to take care of herself. She was furious and retaliated by stripping the house of everything she could manage, even the kids' beds. I was dumbfounded and couldn't figure out how on earth she could do this to her own kids. For me it was déjà vu.

It should have been at this point that I realized she would probably persist and should have walked away, but I loved those kids and really did care for Arthur. We had become incredibly good friends.

So Pastor Lewis suggested we have a betrothal ceremony and move in together to save on my rent and use my furnishings to help replenish what she had taken from the house. I told him I had never heard of a betrothal and he explained it was an old tradition dating back to Bible days.

This is great. God really allows this! Arthur said he would support us and wanted me to drop out of college, fix up the house, and watch the kids. I decided to trust him since he was such a smart man. Love isn't everything. I would learn to love him as my grandmother had learned when she embarked on an arranged marriage to my grandfather. *Love was a choice we made. Not a feeling!*

Art had an excellent job and the plan was to support us all. I took care of the house and the kids, except for Alan. He was on his own or with his grandmother most of the time. I spent time with Art's mother. We went out together and we both loved to go to rug hooking classes; it was fun. Arthur was her only child and she had him later in life, so she was close to my grandmother's age and they became friends, as well.

We wanted to get married but he wasn't divorced yet. So we did as the pastor suggested and had a betrothal ceremony. He had convinced us it was

Not in the fire

biblical. The betrothal was in 1987 and the divorce finally happened too, but with lots of difficulties. We endured years of his ex-wife's behaviors, to include stalking us and daily harassing phone calls. We had to get new locks on the doors as well as an alarm system and an answering machine.

I sensed his ex-wife sat in the courthouse seeking ideas for charges she could file against us, civil or criminal. She amassed quite an array of ways we were negligent from bad water to my supposed attempt to kill her. She claimed she saw me outside of her house with a gun. When the police responded to that particular complaint, they arrived at our house to find us all sitting in our pj's watching TV. It was clear she was losing it. I didn't own a gun at the time.

Our life together was a journey of disruptions. The kids and Arthur would rally around me, asking me to not let her scare me away. So I hung on and prayed. Because of the betrothal, there also were allegations of bigamy. I guess it was a mixed blessing that there was nothing legal about the betrothal, as I now know. Bonnie and Frankie, and others as well, encouraged us to hang in there. They surmised it would stop after a while but it never did. She was the only one at the time who was trying to break us up. It was a new start for us both and I felt God was with us. ("I am born of God and the evil one the devil cannot touch me." 1 John 5:18) Still lots to learn.

Arthur told me one night he couldn't sleep with me when we got married because he was afraid I would get pregnant and, as he said, "go bonkers like his ex-wife." He claimed she had gotten increasingly more disturbed after each child. "I never did with Tonna," I told him. But he said I had to get "fixed;" he didn't trust any other way. I now wonder why on earth I didn't tell *him* to get "fixed," or why he didn't arrive at that decision on his own, especially since he contended that none of the births were planned; they "had to" marry after he had gotten drunk at a graduation party and they slept together.

I thought about it and realized we had four children between us and that should be enough. So I was scheduled for a partial hysterectomy. Who shows up at the hospital? Thomas! He was upset and said, "Don't do this. You know how badly you want kids." I said, "Are we going to get back together?" He said, "No." I replied, "Then I'm not waiting. Arthur wants this." Thomas' mother, Dottie, had called me a few times trying to get me not to date him because of his ex-wife, and again when she found out that he insisted that I have this surgery. What is wrong with me? I'll tell you I left God's Word out of my life during this time. I believed what people said, even when, deep down, I realized it was wrong!

This was not going to be easy; I knew that. I also knew that it might not work. His ex-wife was obsessed with our plans to marry. She was relentless, hateful, jealous, and so spiteful. I should have asked to move away. The court costs mounted and the headaches never stopped, but I felt needed by the kids, Arthur, and his mother.

Because of Arthur's mother's pleas that I reconsider, Betty and the kids touched my heart and unknowingly compelled me to hang in there. They not only seemed to love Tonna and me, but also I was convinced they needed me. They tended to cling to me as if they might lose me every time we got together, probably due to their mother's taunts that she would get me to leave sooner or later. I pitied their insecurity and I didn't have the heart to disappoint them. They definitely grew on me.

So I decided we were going to do this and God would help us all, but I never asked God if He wanted this. I had become accustomed to act on my own. Weren't kids, even children of God, supposed to make their own decisions at some point in life? I found out the answer is, "No, never without GOD!" *When was this harassment going to end? Will God help us to get through this?* The answer was, "Yes, He did, as long as we put Him first." I prayed with the kids for her to find God and for us all to get along. ("… but one thing I do: forgetting what lies behind, and straining forward to what lies ahead," Philippians 3:13)

[**Author's note:** *Why didn't I see that God was using them to get me to wake up! I can approach God with boldness, freedom and confidence. (Ephesians 3:12) Why didn't I ask God first? I was acting on my own. I would show my Father I could make good choices, yet was this one? I was going through so much and I was not sure how this was going to work, but I decided one day at a time would be best. Arthur and I became good friends and he called at lunchtime every day. Once a week we had a date night. We did things with the kids. We all kept praying that his ex-wife would get a life that didn't include us. Yet, she never did.*]

Chapter 28

My Last Marriage--For Better or Worse

W e were legally married in 1989. Despite the rocky start, there was so much about our relationship and the marriage that made it seem like we were a perfect fit. The kids got along great, we all worked well together, and one would never know I wasn't their mom. We enjoyed the same things. Life was good and full of fun activities. They even asked to call me Mom, which incited more hatred toward me from their birth mother.

I did earn a little extra money by caring for his Aunt Betty, a wonderful woman, who was suffering from emphysema, as well as caring for his mother. For six years, Betty H. suffered with Alzheimer's. I used my salaries to fix up the house and landscape around the house. It was a big house, and he had bought out his ex-wife's share from her. I finished parts of the house that had not been completed and renovated parts that needed work. I was a stay-at-home mom and care provider for both Bettys. At times, Betty W. needed us to spend the night; she was afraid to be alone. She couldn't breathe well, even on an oxygen tank. So Tonna and AJ and I took turns. This went on for three years. I was back and forth. We agreed she didn't need to worry about paying me. In front of me, she called her brother, who was executor of her estate, and said when she died he was to pay me all the money I'd earned out of her estate.

We were invited to parties thrown by the business where he worked, and one of the men he worked with was Bill and his wife, Lana, who was one of the wait staff driven nearly mad by MJ's antics while we enjoyed ice cream back when we first met. Bill asked us to check out his church and so we did. The kids were so excited to have a different church; they loved absolutely everything about it. I was too.

Arthur had never heard a message like the one we heard at our new church. We made friends and got involved in activities at the church, and so did the kids. Weekends were set aside to have fun, but they had to go to their biological mom's house every other weekend. As an additional form of harassment, she did her best to demand changes in visits.

The calls from his ex-wife to Arthur were innumerable. Eventually he slammed down the phone after each of her harassing calls. He didn't share the things she said to him. In all of this, I tried to make the environment as peaceful as I could for the children. Arthur would go for a ride after many of her calls and come back when he calmed down. The kids would cry, "Why doesn't she leave us alone?"

I overheard AJ singing "drop dead mother" songs in the shower. It broke my heart. *Why would a mother do this to her kids? Why can't she just enjoy her visits and be happy that they are loved and cared for?* She was a smart woman and she could have done so many good things for them. It was beyond my understanding then and still is now.

Shortly after this time, Betty W. died. I was looking forward to the money I had earned watching Betty W. One day, her brother called and said we were going to court and not to say anything; he'd be sure to compensate me. So I sat in the courtroom and said nothing. Later, Arthur got a call and he agreed with her brother that the amount I earned was too high; one-quarter of it was good enough. I was hurt, upset. What right did he have to say my three years was not worth what I asked for? Thirty thousand dollars was what I asked for, for around the clock care for three years; her fourth year was in a rest home. I didn't even change what it would have cost. She had agreed on the price. Her brother just wanted the money for himself. I was so upset. I got a check for ten thousand dollars; that was it. I spent that much on her care.

One day, AJ had a breakdown in the car on her way to a visit with her mom. She insisted she couldn't go. We stopped the car and I got into the back seat and held her. I asked if she would like to get away for the weekend with Tonna and me. She loved the idea.

Arthur called her mom and told her that AJ got sick in the car and wasn't well enough to visit. I packed the car and we took off to Weirs Beach in New Hampshire for two days. We slept in the station wagon. No one bothered us. In fact, the police watched over us. We went swimming at night and watched the boats go by. We laughed and spent the day on the board

Not in the fire

walk. AJ and I had a long talk about issues with our mothers. I understood. I told her we could not help them, other than to pray for them and take one day at a time. If at any time things got out of hand at home, the chief of police was nearby. We knew him well; he even attended our new church.

I understood how hard this was for them because there were times when I didn't think I could cope, but I tried to help them deal with it the only way I knew how. We can't change a person but we can pray and try to adjust.

That said, it was around this time that MJ was taken from school by his mother without our knowing. To say I was worried is an understatement and Arthur was angry more than anything. We called the police and she was summoned to court, yet she wasn't ordered to bring him home until after the court date. We were not allowed to see him until then because she had filed a charge that I was abusive to MJ, which was absurd. We won our case. She lost some visiting time because of her actions and was ordered to have counseling.

During the time MJ was with his mom he became sick at school. The school office called me and said I needed to see MJ because he was a wreck. I responded immediately, and they provided a private room where we wouldn't be seen together. MJ cried as soon as he saw me and sat on my lap. I held him for twenty minutes while he cried and I tried to comfort him. No one ever mentioned this visit. I told MJ it was going to be okay and to just hang in there. I told him to run to the police department if it got too bad and ask for the chief of police in our town, who was familiar with the many incidents caused by MJ's mom.

The school allowed him to call me every day until the court date. Though it worked out, MJ never seemed to rid himself of the fear that she could take him again. She filed with the court to force us to bring him for visits, but the judge chose to talk to MJ alone in his chambers. It became obvious to the judge that MJ was traumatized by what happened and said he was not going to make a thirteen-year-old boy visit under those circumstances. The judge promised to revisit the case if MJ became comfortable with his mother again.

To keep things in balance, we had family prayer time on Mondays, attended Wednesday night youth group, attended family functions on Saturday, went to church on Sunday, had family fun on Sunday afternoons, and attended Sunday evening services, as well. If the church was open, we were there as a family. I went to all of the kids' games—lacrosse, volleyball, etc. Those who pray together stay together! I held on to that.

Arthur and I served as secretaries for the senior group at church and attended trips with them. We started a marriage group for couples with the clear statement that it was as much for us as it was for any other couple. I felt we had a good marriage, yet we freely acknowledged everyone can benefit from information on making relationships stronger. There was a nice group of about eight couples. We focused on various video series and discussions. We also had our Friday night prayer meeting and Bible study at our house.

About this time, Betty H. was in a rest home and was dying. We all went with our friends, prayed with her, and said our good-byes. She was gone with the Lord. I was glad she was free and did not have to just lay there. She had fallen and broken her hip prior to entering the rest home. We were told there was a tumor on her hip and they had to put her leg on backwards. I thought it would have been better to remove it. She'd never walk again. Besides, Arthur's ex wouldn't let her in; she hated her. Why would she want her around now? She even stole Betty's wedding band, which MJ found on the floor of her car at his next visit; he brought it to me. Betty's freedom was also less stress for all of us.

My brother had remarried and lived close to us when I was married to Thomas. He was diagnosed with bipolar disorder and had big issues, much like Mom. Nearly every time he and his wife had a baby, they left them with us soon after weaning. If my mom came for a weekend, she would help care for them, but we cared for them on weekdays most of the time; we always took them with us to church on Sundays.

After my surgery I had dead baby dreams. In the dreams, babies screamed at me that I killed them. These dreams occurred for few years.

Having Brian's babies to care for actually made those dreams go away. Thus, our family steadily grew from three or four kids to six or seven kids at times. We got a station wagon to fit everyone and we were happy. Alan even said to me once, "Thank you for making this house a home!"

Brian's issues went beyond our caring for his babies, though. One day he came to the house screaming that he wanted his kids. I took him for a walk by the pond near our house to talk and calm him down. MJ and Arthur stood on our porch. They were scared for me, but I put my hand up and told them to stay put. Brian was yelling that he gave birth to them and if he wanted to kill them, it was his choice and he could kill me in one chop. He could. It's not a good thing when someone with his instability has a black belt, which he earned when he was married to his first wife.

God has given me peace in many emergency situations, and He did this time. I just looked up at Brian and said with tears in my eyes, "If that's what you want to do and face God with it, go for it." He froze and stared at me. I looked into his eyes, and he turned and left, saying nothing. I told him as he walked to the car that I would always be there for him. I assured him that I loved him and God had me watch his kids, but I was not taking them away. I was helping them be safe when he was not doing well. He looked at me from his car and drove off. Arthur and MJ were shocked as I walked by them into the house and said, "It's over. Let's just get the kids to bed." We had a Friday Bible study after kids went to bed. Erv Maleta, a great chaplain and pastor, was the leader. He was moving and asked if we could continue the Bible study at our home. We said yes, and di so for almost six years.

Nancy, a friend from church, and a couple from the study group, asked if we could invite a new couple, Rick and Samantha (Sam) to our Friday study, and I said, "Why not?"

So Rick and Sam joined our group. The group had a progressive dinner, where each course was hosted by a different household, and one of the courses was at the home of this new couple. Soon they asked us to move the meeting to their house. At first, I didn't understand the reason for the request, nor did I feel right about it, but we did. It created a hardship for us to leave the six kids. Sam's mother lived with them and had numerous medical problems and I know how hard that was. Slowly, others just stopped coming; it didn't work for them since they lived closer to our house than the new venue. A few dropped off because they didn't feel comfortable in this couple's home. In the end, the meetings simply ceased.

We should have just moved it back to our place. This was a study that started at Pastor Maleta's house and then moved to our home when they departed. It had been going for six years at this point. We initially voted on a break from the meetings and we never came back together from that break. ("Let not your hearts be troubled, neither let them be afraid." John 14:27a)

During this time, there was another event that was exciting. In a dream, I was told to go to the Rowe conference center. They had an elder from a Native American tribe scheduled to speak. He was not being treated properly because they didn't understand his customs. All elders expect a guide to be assigned to them. He was waiting in his room for one but none came.

So I got up early, set everyone up for the day, and told Arthur what I was told to do. He said to go for it. He had met my native family on two reserves so he was understanding of their customs and what they meant to me. He attended events with me at times. We even had a native wedding ceremony after the betrothal and our wedding. He married me three times in all. We also had a vow renewal, so he made the promises to me a total of four times!

I found Black Elk in his room waiting for someone to accompany him to breakfast and also for someone to carry his materials for him throughout the day. I told him God sent me to help him. At first he just stared at me, then he said, "That is nice. Tell your God thank you." I spent the day helping him. His nephew was attending but it was not his responsibility to help carry things. He had his own role in the conference. I watched people ask who I was. He answered, "Her God has sent her to help because no one here came to help."

Participants made and entered a sweat lodge. It was my first one ever and I started to panic. It was so hot I could not breathe. Black Elk reached out to me and touched my hand. He said, "All is good!" I calmed down and was fine. I asked the management where he should go for supper and they said meals were not served at night. I thought that was strange and asked where they expected him to eat when he had no car. They offered no solutions, so I called Arthur and asked if they could come to the house for supper. The kids were excited and Arthur agreed, so I invited them to our house for supper and a nice evening. We prayed and Black Elk and his nephew listened. I took them back to their rooms for the night.

It is true that he is a shaman, but God loves him too. He asked if I would come back the next day. Arthur said I could. They came to our house again that evening since the conference didn't provide supper; the conference center had no idea how disrespectful that was. I asked about transporting him to the airport and they said he had to rent a car. Even Arthur knew it was wrong to treat an honored guest in that way, so we took them to the airport.

The conference center didn't offer us anything. Before he left that second night, Black Elk signed my copy of the book he had written. He sent me a copy to show them he was warning them; it was his way of honoring me. He asked me for an object on my prayer table where I had placed items of importance to me. I agreed and he said he liked my brad ties and could he trade mine for his. I was honored and said, "Sure." In a picture in his second book he is wearing my brad ties.

He let us pray for them before they left. He seemed interested in my God. For a long time, I prayed he would accept the Lord before he died. He was in his eighties at the time I met him. I prayed for all my native family. He

Not in the fire

mailed me a copy of the book with a note saying he was seeking to learn more about my God.

Sam and Rick became close friends to us. Our kids were best friends and our daughter AJ began dating their older son. Sam, the wife, used to sit and play cribbage with Arthur in their dining room and her husband played the guitar with the kids and me at the far end of house so as not to be too loud. We loved singing songs together.

I began to think of Sam as a best friend and very much like a sister. I would have done most anything for her. They asked us to go to their island on vacation with them. On the way to join them, we hit a big pheasant. We stopped on the side of the road and I pulled it out of the grill. "Supper," I said. We all laughed. People at church told me to be careful of her friendship, yet they couldn't explain why. I felt she was lonely and just needed a friend.

We arrived on the island and transferred our belongings from the car to a boat. We had our own cabin, and while the boys played by the shore, we unpacked the boat. The girls had stayed home from this trip for various reasons. There was family around at home so the girls would have supervision.

The men and boys took a walk around the island then went out on the boat. Sam was in the cabin occupied by her mother when all of a sudden I heard a scream. I ran to their cabin. Sam's mom had her hands around Sam's neck and was trying to strangle her. Sam was starting to get pale at this point. I thought she would soon pass out. It took me a few minutes, but I got her to let go. The mother kept saying horrible things about Sam that made no sense to me, repeating she was evil.

Sam was embarrassed and said that it was over and she was safe I could go. I wandered to where there would be a campfire and sat down. When Rick came back with the boys, I told him about Sam and her mom and asked, "Where is Arthur?"

Rick said Arthur decided to stay in the cabin, so he went alone with the boys. He left to see what was going on in his cabin with Sam 's mother. Eventually they came out of their cabin, and I asked if Dot was okay. I offered to cook supper for her but Sam answered she was cooking up my bird for me and they would have hotdogs. She said to just relax by the fire. So I joined the others, and we all talked. Arthur finally showed up from somewhere, not the direction of our cabin. He was quiet and Sam was acting strangely. So far, everything was strange, and I was sure I had no clue what was going on. *Should we leave tomorrow*, I asked myself. I wish we had.

Not in the fire

Sam appeared with the food about an hour later and we all ate. I became tired, so I said good night and went to bed. I told MJ to not stay up too late. About two hours later, MJ came in to go to bed and said his prayers with me. He asked if I was okay and I had to admit I wasn't feeling very well. I had a fever and cramps and I was dizzy. I prayed silently, *Lord, help me, please!*

Around eleven I had to go to the bathroom. I was hanging onto things as I worked my way through the cabin. MJ was sleeping. I looked for my husband but I didn't see him. I noticed Rick out on the point by the shore playing his guitar and I could tell he was alone.

I went around to the other side of the cabin to go to the outhouse. I saw motion in the other cabin window. Sam was watching, but as I turned to wave, she shut the curtain. I was hoping she would help me, but she didn't, though I was sure she must have seen me. I wondered, *but where is Arthur?*

I was in that outhouse for a quite a while. I saw no one on my way back to our cabin. Rick was still out on the point but was too far away to call for the help I sensed I needed. I didn't want to wake the boys. I managed to get to our cabin and it was late when Arthur came to bed. I tried to talk to him but he had turned his back to me and lay on his good ear; he couldn't hear me. I was miserable all night and was fitful, but finally fell asleep. I awoke very thirsty and all alone.

Arthur and MJ were gone. I was so sick that I couldn't move. I just lay there in pain. This went on all day and through the evening. No one checked in on me at all. *Why?* They came to bed late again that night, and in the morning, when I didn't come out again, Rick insisted that he, Arthur and MJ check on me to see how I was. They brought a walking stick they had made. When Rick saw me, he said, "Wow! Arthur, help me get her outside. She's so pale and she looks really sick." So they got me out of the cabin and into a chair on the beach near the fire pit. It was sunny and the heat felt good. Rick asked what I needed. MJ was worried and asked if I was okay. He said he was going to check on me but said his dad told him to let me sleep.

I told Rick I needed my medicine kit from our car. Arthur started swearing. I hadn't known him to swear before. He said, "What the blank-blank-blank do you expect me to do, walk on water? The tide's gone out and it's not deep enough for a boat." Rick looked shocked. Sam looked weird and walked toward their cabin. Rick spoke up again and said, "I can take you over, it's not that low yet. We need to leave now though." ("The Lord will fulfill his purpose for me; your steadfast love, O Lord, endures forever. Do not forsake the work of your hands." Psalm 138:8)

Not in the fire

Arthur looked annoyed and said, "I guess it's ok if you say so." Sam had hung back from going into the cabin. She got angry and said, "No. You can't leave me alone with my mom." Rick said to just leave her in her room until he got back in a couple of hours and just lock the door. Before he left he said to Sam, "Don't let Barb sit in the sun too long. Help her move to the shade so she doesn't get heat stroke or a bad sunburn."

Sam grumbled something and left. The boys were playing by the beach. Sam went into the house and I have never understood why she never came out to talk to me, bring me my water, or get me out of the sun. What kind of friend did I have? I was too weak to move by myself. I tried but I couldn't stand. The boys disappeared onto the other side of the island, presumably to look around, so I fell asleep in the chair.

When I awoke, Rick was standing over me. He was mad. I was burned to a crisp and he said I needed a hospital badly but there wasn't any way to get there until morning when the tide came back in.

The symptoms of sunstroke were added to the symptoms that had made me ill in the first place. I felt like I was dying. Rick got me water and I took the medicine they had retrieved for me. Within an hour I was feeling a little bit better. Rick gave me something to eat. I didn't know where Arthur was; Sam was nowhere to be seen either. I was confused and worried about what on earth was going on with me. Rick asked MJ to help me to the cabin. I slept. Arthur and Rick helped me up in the morning, and I felt somewhat better. I didn't remember Arthur coming to bed or getting up. I heard MJ come to bed. He had said good night and he hoped I would be okay. He said he would pray for me. They finally gave me lots to drink. The sunburn pain took over as the intensity of the illness subsided.

I concluded I must have caught a flu bug, yet it felt so different to me. I considered food poisoning, but that made no sense since no one else got sick. They all tasted the bird.

By the afternoon, I was able to get up by myself. Still, I was not feeling well and I suggested we leave. Arthur wasn't happy. He showed no concern for me, but Rick insisted he needed to get me to a doctor. So Rick packed the boat and took me and our stuff across to our car. I sat on a rock with our belongings and waited alone for the others to come, too. Arthur hadn't come with us but waited for the next trip across, even though it was a half hour each way and I would be alone for that amount of time.

A storm came out of nowhere just as Arthur and MJ got in the boat. As they continued toward me, I could see the waves were frightening MJ.

Not in the fire

When they came into view, I could see him beginning to panic more. Without thinking, I raised my hands and shouted, "In Jesus' name, be still." MJ calmed down as the waves stilled. When Rick was almost to the other side returning to the island, the waves started to roil again. I asked, "Lord, please keep it calm until Rick gets to the other shore." He did. After he was safe, the storm picked up again. I was pleased to see he was safely on the other side. We loaded our big Buick. I couldn't wait to get home. ("Call to me and I will answer you." Jeremiah 33:3)

Arthur said nothing on the way home. For the next three years of our marriage, he didn't have relations with me and he rarely spoke to me. He was frequently angry, and he disappeared for hours at a time with no explanation. When I asked about his anger or his mood, he either blamed it on his ex-wife or mumbled something I couldn't understand. He took a new quality assurance job in Maine and often was on the road for weeks at a time.

I was left to deal with all of the children and their needs by myself, as well as his ex-wife's harassment. I called him each evening to find out how things were going and chat for a few minutes. He wouldn't talk for long and he always said, "Goodbye." Previously he had always said, Goodbye and I love you." He never said, "Good night" or "I love you" anymore." It was a hard time for me and the kids; we did not understand what was wrong with him.

Often, he had Rick come and do odd jobs for us around the house when he was away. He said it was because they needed extra money for Sam's cancer med; she fought cancer for years. Rick and I would have been alone in the house if Tonna hadn't been home nearly all of the time. Otherwise, it seems as though it wasn't a good idea. As long as Tonna was there, I invited him to have lunch or coffee on the porch. Probably it was inevitable that we started to share and talk about our marriages.

We became good friends; we were concerned about Arthur and Sam. They were both acting strangely. Once we started comparing notes, we were uncomfortable with our suspicions. Sam seemed to be away from home visiting her sister often. We decided to pay close attention and I sent Rick on a weeklong trip with Arthur to see what he could find out. He found out nothing. During the week they were away, I tried to get closer to Sam, too, but she wouldn't talk to me.

When Rick and Arthur came home, Rick and I decided to go to the pastor together to talk about what we should do. Pastor advised us to stop talking to one another about our marriages and pray for each other's marriages instead. "Leave it to God," he said. He warned us that they would accuse us if we continued to share this bond that was centered on finding out what was going on with our spouses. We followed his advice.

However, Arthur asked Rick to cut some trees for us because Sam insisted they needed the money for new tires. I knew nothing about it so I was surprised to see him when he arrived on our property. When he told me what he was doing, I said to go ahead but asked if it would take long. I guess I acted weird and he was concerned, so he simply set out to cut the tree.

I had planned on taking my life that day and had not planned on company. I invented something for Tonna and all the kids to do so that she wasn't home. Rick was unexpected. I watched him from my window, hoping he would hurry up and get everything done. As I watched, he put down the saw and came barging into the house. "Listen," he said, "we've been friends for a few years now. What's up? I'm not moving until you tell me. I can feel something's wrong!"

I broke down and admitted what I had planned to do. He threw out the poison mushroom soup I had made. He told me all about his life, from his failed first marriage to his current marriage to Sam, and how God got him through it all. He said, "We can't take our own life." He wrote out the prayer he recited two or three times each day. It was beautiful; I still have it and recite it. He made me promise that I wouldn't do anything to harm myself ever again and to call him if I felt that way again.

He admitted that he knew the pastor was right and that we were getting too close. They would try to make this about us and we couldn't let them do that and ruin our walk with the Lord. I agreed.

Then I felt led to get a basin of water and wash his feet. I told him I would never stop praying for his marriage and happiness. I told him I prayed that Sam would learn to love him and see what a great husband she had, and I would never do anything to harm myself. I told him I would get help from my doctor. He surprised me and washed my feet as well. He promised to do all he could to help Arthur realize how lucky he was to have me and he would pray for our marriage to get back what we had in the past and for Arthur's ex-wife to leave us alone. Besides an occasional telephone call to check on my well-being, we only spoke in person at church, and just to say hello.

Sam and Arthur had an argument at church the following Sunday. They stood away from the crowd at the back corner of the church, but it was obvious to me there was a disagreement. I decided to be bold and ask her what it was about. She said she was trying to get Arthur to sit with me in church and not in the back, but the following week she visited the pastor and said her husband and I had shared too much and we couldn't talk to each other any longer. I'm not sure how she knew that, other than from Arthur. She also wanted Anthony to stop calling her son, and that Rick and Arthur shouldn't be friends. It was weird, hurtful, and difficult to know what to do, but the pastor helped me to deal with it and I had friends who encouraged me to let go and let God work. So I did.

People started talking. They were making up their own versions of what was going on.

With Arthur sitting in the back of church rather than with me, the talk became all about us. Sam knew what she was crafting. Arthur stopped coming to church. MJ would no longer attend if he couldn't talk with their son.

I started spending much more time with God. I was trying to move on. I felt led to do one more thing. I gave money to our pastor to send Arthur, MJ, Rick and his son to Promise Keepers. Sam got so mad, but Pastor said it would be good for them to heal and that God wanted to restore their relationships, and that this separation she wanted was not going to be forever. Healing had to happen. They went, but when they got home, nothing was different. I had tried to visit Sam and talk about what was the problem. Before she slammed the door in my face, she said "You don't know who you're dealing with." I was stunned and hurt. *What does that mean? What was I missing in all this?* I'm sure now that I see who I'm dealing with. Satan is in charge here!

[**Author's note:** *As a family, we were immersed not just in church life, but also in prayers and devotions at home. Why did this havoc fall on me? Why was there an ex-wife who continually harassed all of us? It isn't evident from this chapter narrative how long we had been close to our friends who owned the island in Maine. It had been over three years that we had been so close, as close as sisters, I thought. Sam's mom called me her daughter. We were with each other so much that we had talked about selling our homes and getting an apartment building so that we all could live together.*]

Chapter 29

The Late Hellish Honeymoon

Isought help from our pastor on more than one occasion. I had spoken about the fact that we never got to take our honeymoon. I had saved for years so that we could go after we renewed our vows and the kids were older. The pastor said the timing might be right at this time. "Why don't you take him on that nice, long honeymoon you've always wanted?" So, I planned a month- long trip to the Bahamas with some money I had saved from caring for Arthur's aunt and Betty, his mother. Our friends and our pastor encouraged Arthur to go. He had started coming back to church and even sat with me after his trip to Promise Keepers, but he was never the same man I married. Something had happened, but what?

And the trip was a nightmare. He did everything from making fun of me, saying I was ugly, fat, had bulging eyes, anything that crossed his mind, to criticizing my lack of coordination. But most of the time, I was simply ignored, and he wasn't even reacting to all the beauty around us. People stared at him weirdly. The guides kept asking me if I was safe. What were they seeing that I didn't want to see? He said, "I'm going off for the rest of the day; you can do whatever you want."

There was no connection nor an opportunity to grow in our relationship. It all backfired. During the few times we spent together in a mutual activity, he became snide about every little thing I did. I forced myself to try to cheer up, swimming with the dolphins, sitting on the beautiful beach, and walking around buying things for all the kids. We did go on a glass bottom boat and saw all the fish under our feet, including sharks. I thought it was cool and scary at the same time, but he sat across from me, not next to me.

Not in the fire

We ate shark meat for lunch. I threw it up because it was so salty. He wasn't very sympathetic and just laughed at me. I was in a deep depression when I got back on the boat to our destination in Florida. I looked at the ocean and took in comforting thoughts of jumping in and ending it all. I could hear the waves calling me to join them and find peace.

I decided to put down all I was feeling in a note. When I gave it to Arthur, thinking he would care, he threw it on the boat deck. He then went back to the lounge chair, covered his head with the day's newspaper, and took a snooze. One of the ship's employees saw me crying, picked up the note, read it, and put me on suicide watch. "You can't be jumping overboard. Everything will be okay."

They were concerned with Arthur's reaction. When we got to shore, they asked if I was safe with my husband. I was shocked at the question. I admitted he wasn't showing that he cared, but I was confident he would never hurt me. *But would he?* I thought.

We visited our friends Ken and Nancy in Florida. Nancy was the friend who introduced us to Rick and Sam. Ken was working a temporary job in Florida and they were staying in a hotel.

They took us to a beautiful botanical garden. They noticed something was off and Nancy asked if Arthur was okay. I admitted that I wasn't sure. The Florida sun was really hot, and I fell asleep in a lounge chair when we returned to our hotel. I was burned to a crisp in the sun again. It was too much for my fair skin. I wondered why Arthur didn't wake me up; he knew I burned easily.

I had to go to the hospital clinic and they gave me a shot and told him to apply a topical cream on my burn three times a day. The orders were for me to rest for a few days and drink lots of water. We returned to our hotel.

Arthur didn't help me at all. I spent two days alone in the hotel room and he went sightseeing. He didn't help with the cream and I had to do the best I could alone. And I took cold baths. I didn't eat for two days and he never offered to get anything for me. I fasted and prayed.

When I recovered, we went to Disney World, though I could hardly move. I enjoyed the park, despite my physical and emotional pain. He didn't want to ride on the same attractions I wanted, so we split up. We met at the exit at the close of the day. *Why on earth is he so cold to me?*

The ride home seemed longer than ever since he wasn't talking. All I could do was listen to the radio. Soon after we returned home, we had a family trip planned. All of the kids were planning to go with us along with

Not in the fire

AJ's fiancé. Danny was such a sweet guy. I was so glad AJ had found him through her friend in college. Our lodging was a nice condo with large windows, and once again, Arthur ignored me. I still felt sick from the sunburn. Tonna was the only one worried about me. The others were busy having fun together.

When we returned home from the family vacation, I finally told him I couldn't go on like this any longer. I insisted, "We need to meet with the pastor and you need to seek help for your anger and whatever is bothering you. Or I want a divorce." All he heard was that I wanted a divorce. He had an iron rake in his hand and he swung it at me. It came within a fraction of hitting me in the face. The gouge is still in the bedroom door where the rake connected.

I was frozen. I didn't freak out or respond at all. It's like Jesus was in control. I was calm. It was God, not me. Arthur became more agitated and redder in the face. He sat down in our bathroom on the toilet and I thought he was having a stroke. I asked if he was alright and he grabbed the rake, went outside, and beat that rake into the side of the house. Then he drove off. ("And the peace of God, which passes all understanding, will guard your hearts and minds in Christ Jesus." Philippians 4:7)

While he was gone, I called the pastor to tell him what happened. The pastor told me to call the police and have him arrested for attempting to kill me. But I couldn't do it. I feared MJ would leave with him, and I didn't want to lose MJ. He was only sixteen at the time, and I couldn't risk messing him up at that point in his life. He had been through enough and meant so much to me. He was already questioning his faith.

Tonna helped me move Arthur0's belongings into the basement and put a lock on my door. Poor Tonna had watched the whole thing. I had to reassure her she wasn't in danger and not to be upset. "God will protect you just the way He protected me." She believed that. ("May the God of hope fill you with all joy and peace in believing ..." Romans 15:13a)

Arthur came home and the only thing he could say was, "You're not going to lock me out of my bedroom forever!" No, "I'm sorry." Nothing. Then he headed to the basement room where there was a bed, love seat, and TV for him. I stayed in my room for the next two years and he ignored me the whole time.

He went once to the pastor, who told him he needed to show some affection. Arthur's only idea of affection at that point was sex. I had lost fifty pounds and I did look good. He thought because we hadn't been intimate for so long that it was my only problem. By then, that was the last thing on my mind.

I pushed him away and said, "I'm not going to be treated like a whore. You can't just jump on me and think it's all better. We have a lot to work on before we get to that point again. Remember what our relationship was like when we first met? That is what I want!"

He said, "Well, we're not going to do counseling since it didn't work."

"It didn't work because you won't acknowledge how bad this is. You need to tell the truth. How did we get to this? I have given you all I have to give. I've tried to be the best wife and mother I could. I cared for your mother and aunt. What more do you want?"

He didn't answer my question directly. He said, "Nothing. You're right, but all it does is make me feel more inadequate, because I can't love you like you love me. I don't feel it. I don't know how to love. I just haven't ever felt like that."

I still didn't know why. I said, "What happened?"

He just looked down and walked away. I was so confused. What had gone wrong?

Arthur filed for divorce. I worried about what I was going to do. I imagined that I would have to leave because it was his house.

I always felt that if he left, he would come back after he worked out whatever was bothering him. My girlfriend Lana thought he was just going through a change of life that some men go through. I never asked for anything and I never got a lawyer. I was naïve. I found out that I needed one when it was too late. I really thought he would come around.

I was so despondent that I went into the woods and cried while lying in the snow. I imagined freezing like the Native Americans did in the old days. I prayed tearfully. ("… praying at all times." Ephesians 6:18a) After a good amount of time, I was freezing and falling asleep. An angel came to me and told me to get up and go back into the house and said, *Tell him that if he wants the divorce, he has to be the one to leave.* You're not going anywhere. ("He [Elijah] came to a broom tree, sat down under it and prayed that he might die. 'I have had enough, LORD'." 1 Kings 19:4 (NIV))

God said to me, *It is not your time.* This was the second time He had said this to me in my life. I just answered, *Lord, please go before me. I can't do this alone.* He answered, You have never been alone! You just chose to not listen at times. I replied, *I am so sorry. Forgive me!*

So I went back into the house and told Arthur. I explained all that had happened. He looked at me for a moment and said, "Fine, I will leave. I'll start looking for a place." *Wow*, I thought.

Added to my agony was my concern about MJ, who by now was just turning seventeen. He was so confused and doing badly in school. I didn't know what to do. I said things I regret to him out of my confused state.

So much had happened and I was not myself. I had lost weight and was still suffering from the effects of a car accident that occurred a few months before when the roads were snow-covered and slippery. I was stopped at an intersection when a town-owned truck rammed the rear of my car and shoved me into the intersection. Thank God nothing was coming. Both Tonna and I were hurt and we had to see a doctor, followed by a chiropractor. I needed the help of a lawyer in order to get our medical bills covered. In all of this, Arthur showed no concern.

I still didn't get a lawyer about the divorce. I was distressed, on medications, seeing a therapist, but still not dealing well with any of it. Folks at church were worried about me; many asked if I was okay? "No, I'm not," I'd answer, "My life is falling apart, and I don't know why!" *What did I do wrong? He's married me four times before Christ and vowed to love me. Was it all fake?*

I held out hope that Arthur would love me as he had in the past. So that I could keep an eye on MJ and to help until Arthur came around, I bought a mobile home for them a short distance from the house. I paid for it and for the first year's association fees out of my savings. I also gave him half the furnishings from the house. "Why?" he asked. "I want you both to be okay," I told him. I bought him a washer and dryer and whatever I could think of to help them get set up. I also spent a good deal of time and effort to get the place cleaned up. He never said thank you. MJ did.

The mobile home idea wasn't as helpful as I had hoped. Arthur was seldom there; he stayed in Vermont where he worked. The few times MJ visited, he became distressed and the visits ceased. He had asked me to give him driving lessons and I was rash and foolish in my sarcastic suggestion that he should ask his mom. I regret that so very much; I turned him away just as he was reaching out to me. Why on earth did I do that? His birth mother was saying things to confuse him and his sister AJ, as well.

Arthur never came by and in a short time he sold the mobile home. In the end, MJ moved in with his birth mother after breaking his leg in a skiing accident. He hated being there alone. It should come as no shock that Arthur moved in with a girlfriend he met at work. I do believe they knew each other before she started working there. Or did they? She was supposed to be a

Christian, yet she was further fracturing my marriage. We had no chance as long as she pursued him. Out of anger, he said he would find a sugar mamma who had a house and there would be no more giving up his house to a woman.

His ex-wife had gotten a lot of money out of him and she bought a house with it. I asked for nothing, but I got the house because it needed so much done to it before we could sell it. We were told there would be no profit from the sale of the house, given the cost of updating it and paying off the mortgage. The house needed a new furnace and the windows were so old wind came rushing through them. The porch was falling apart, the roof leaked, the leach field had leaked sludge for the past three years. The floors in the back of the house had never been finished, the plumbing was old, the water pump was not working well, and the list kept going. He knew his best bet was to give it to me and he said he believed I'd eventually sell it back to him because I could never afford the upkeep. Little did he know God had plans!

To help me cope with the stress during this time, I decided to resume my love of hunting, which I did with my mom in Vermont and at home in Massachusetts by myself. Pastor got me a rifle with money someone had given him so that he could purchase something special for anyone in need. Pastor knew I needed something to get my mind off my worries, and he loved hunting himself. I would go alone, but not really. I invited Jesus to go with me. I stalked the woods alone with God. And I loved to sit in the woods and take in His creation. It was so relaxing, and it was just what I needed. He would tell me where to go and how to get home. I trusted and obeyed. He knows all. Why would I question him? I was happy our relationship was growing.

Beside the brook one day, He suddenly told me to go home. I was not sure why, so I said, "Oh, please, just a bit more. There's plenty more daylight." But He keep telling me to go home and go no further. I was not sure why and I was a little upset, but I said, "Ok, ok, I'm going home." ("Be still and know I am God." Psalm 46:10)

The next day, the talk of the town was about two drunk hunters caught in the woods who were shooting at anything that moved. The police arrested them about a hundred feet from where I had rested and I had been headed in their direction. I got on my knees and thanked God for saving me. I apologized for arguing and said I would not question Him again.

I don't. God helps me with everything in my life. He explains how to do things I never knew how to do before, whether it's how to run my rototiller, weedwhacker, or directions for other tasks. He points things out, and I listen and learn from the master of all. It is highly recommended. No one should be surprised that God wants to be a part of all we do.

I had a hunting buddy who was an older man named Albry. He thought it was not good for me to go hunting alone so he took me out a few times. I hit my first deer with him. I got so excited that I put my gun down to run to the deer and it jumped up and took off. By the time I retrieved my gun, the deer was long gone. There had been a lot of blood, so we chased the deer for the better part of the rest of the day. We found it lying in a deep ravine. We wanted to get him out, but it was too deep. There was no doubt he was mortally wounded. I was so bummed. Lesson learned. Never put the gun down.

It has always been my wish that Arthur would seek help and ask God to teach him to love me again. I am torn apart wondering if it is that hard to love me? We had many adventures in our marriage and so many were good times.

That has not happened, but I tried to help the kids and take good care of the house, as well. The finances haven't been easy. Arthur thought I would be forced to sell the house back to him. Instead, I fixed many of the items on the list that were wrong with the house. I loved our home and I wanted to keep it in the best shape possible so that when he came home, we would share it together. The Lord provided the way and money to do it all.

And God had plans for me, Tonna, and this house. God has made it our home and He filled our home with joy, and girls! One chapter of my life ended, and another opened up. Things can get better!! MJ once made the comment, "So you're starting all over again." I said, "No, I'm continuing on."

[Author's note: *Of all that I have been through, this might have been the hardest time in my life. Our marriage was supposed to be forever. My brother's children called Arthur dad, and they loved him. Everything changed after the island vacation. I tried to do everything I could for Arthur's family, yet they walked away. How could they do that and never call? They just wiped the slate clean and started over. It was so hurtful and I could not see how I deserved this. But life is seldom fair, nor does it have to make sense. MJ, my sweet little boy, is now grown, has a wife and two kids. They live only fifteen minutes away, but he has no time for me. Yet I keep praying for them. It's all I can do.*]

Chapter 30

Consolation

Despite my inability to conceive again, God gave me many children. I raised Brian's children until Arthur left. For a while, I was just a wreck. It was just me and Tonna. I made my life about living for the Lord and taking care of those who needed me. I supported myself by caring for the elderly and taking on cleaning jobs. I had a daycare for about five years after Arthur left, and then I operated a bed and breakfast for three years until 9/11 happened. I then took in two elderly people to care for in my home. I ran an elder day care, plus cared for my own kids for six years, and some of these careers overlapped.

The court ordered Arthur to give me half of his retirement check but he never did. We had purchased a condo share together, which also became mine by court order. Even ownership of the timeshare ended badly. For three years I saved our weeks so that we could spend the whole month of July in Georgia. Folks asked, "Why go to Georgia in July?" My response, "Because that's where and when God told me to go." We saw friends and had a great time. But when we returned home, Arthur informed me that the Holiday Inn had bought out the timeshare and they would not honor my contracted fees. I could no longer afford it. I gave it back to them for free in 2018. So much for my retirement.

Arthur did give me $50 a week for a year and then it stopped. I told him I didn't care. I got the checking account with the highest balance and I lived off that for a little while. I applied for grants and that's how I got a new furnace, septic system, new windows, and roof. The grant money will have to be paid off when I sell, or when I die. I helped pay for Alan and AJ to attend college and I still have the education loans with the house as collateral, but I loved Arthur's kids and I wanted to help them in any way possible.

MJ's mom was able to turn him against me after a short time living with her. She knew how much I loved him and I still miss him. I miss them all. They all are married and each has two children. If Arthur and I had stayed together, I would have all of these grandchildren to cuddle, read to, and otherwise spoil. Most of all, I want to share Jesus with them, but I pray and ask God to take care of them for me.

MJ surprised me one day early on and took me out for Mother's Day at our favorite pizza place. We had a good time. After, he gave me a big hug and said, "I can't be your life." I replied, "I don't expect you to be, but I would like to be a part of your life." He said, "I can't." That was the last time we spoke until AJ's wedding.

I helped financially with AJ's wedding a short time later. I helped her pick out her dress and pay for the church, but the wedding itself was very difficult for me. My family and friends were ignored. We sat by ourselves. I did have a dance with her husband, Danny, who thanked me for raising a good Christian daughter. Alan came up to me and hugged me and said, "I'm sorry for the whole mess my mom's created. She's got issues." However, I tried to tie MJ's bow tie and he turned from me and walked away.

I would like more, but the Lord gives me what I need. I wasn't perfect, but if they could forgive their birth mother years of harassment, headaches, and pranks, an endless list of things, why could they not forgive me of whatever it is that I did?

But there is happiness in what the Lord has given me, my daughters. My guardianship daughters are Mary, Taylor, Rachel, and, of course there is Tonna, who has been there since her birth. In 2021, at her request, I adopted Rachel.

God also provided a way for me to heal from a long-held fear. While visiting a friend at a major medical center, I went to pray in the chapel since only family could visit with the patient. While sitting on the bench, intermittently praying and crying, someone else entered the chapel and sat down across from me. I glanced at him, a man of color. He was close to me and he sensed my discomfort.

Rather than ignore the tension, he addressed it. He came near me and knelt down in front of me and asked if he could pray with me. I said, "Yes, that would be nice." Then he asked if I'd like to talk.

I explained about my experience with what I had seen, which kept me at a distance from anyone of color, even if I had nothing against anyone. God made us all and I ha just been traumatized. And I explained what I thought would happen when white and black folks were together. Memories of the young couple being burned alive were vivid. Words spilled out of my mouth as I explained what I had seen. He assured me he had seen many things in his life, as well. He made it clear to me that the actions of others should in no way define how we feel about each other. He showed sincere sympathy that I witnessed such a horrifying act. He told me he was a pastor and was visiting his mom in the hospital and that she was dying. He said he would pray with me, and he did right then and there. I sense he is still praying for me.

He gave me a Helms Devotional book and asked me to read it. I loved it so much I got the second one. He asked me to wait and he went to get his mother and sisters and introduced them to me. They gave me hugs and sang some songs for me. They had amazing voices. Even his mother was singing in her wheelchair. It was so grand. God's spirit was in the air.

I asked about him at a subsequent visit; they said his mom had died and he returned to Africa. I regretted that I hadn't asked him for his address.

I am able to have some time for myself. I still enjoy the seclusion of hunting; I take no one with me but the Lord. The solitude of the woods is renewing and I have a continuing conversation with the Lord. My brother and I go fishing, which we both enjoyed as youngsters. I enjoy all four of the young women I have raised and who still live with me. The youngest is the closest because she is a lot like me.

God has been so good and present to me in all of my crises. I know I've had times of depression and feeling so unloved, yet I am stronger because of it. Life is better. After a while, I went to an acupuncturist that a friend had seen for years. After my last suicide attempt, he gave me shock therapy. It was great; it re-centered all my energy and all negatives just went away. It's hard to get me riled; I'm much calmer.

Not in the fire

Chapter 31

A Vision from God

I once had a dream about a potter, which is God, who made a teapot and put it on a shelf in his shop. The potter carefully worked on the little pot. Every time a patron came into the shop, the little teapot would reach out and say, "Look up here! Pick me! I'll serve you so well. You might not love me now, but I'll love you enough for both of us."

That characterized most of my relationships with men. I was sure I could love enough for both of us if they would just pick me. I would serve them well and make them glad I was in their lives, just like the little teapot. "I'll take care of you and you will fall in love with me. I know you will. I'll be so good that you can't resist loving me."

People know, and now I know, that it doesn't work that way. My mother thought it worked that way and I took on the same notion. In my dream, the teapot kept being purchased by all of the people in my life. Each one misused it in a different way and eventually the potter would find it in a scrap heap. And He restored it to be used again, each time better than before.

Arthur made the final purchase of the teapot and he threw it away when he no longer wanted it. He destroyed it more than all her life mates; he destroyed her inside and out and destroyed her worth. It seemed beyond repair, and that is how I felt. I thought I looked like trash and was convinced I was useless. I thought that if there was any goodness in me, it was gone.

I recall in the dream the potter's reassurances that he could mend me. I realized the potter represented the Lord, and eventually I could see that He was mending me. It took a long time, but little by little, it happened. My depression began to lift. He reassured me of my worth and that He hadn't given up on me. At the same time, He was going to put me back on the back of the shelf where I couldn't be seen. In the vision, He put me through the fire. He added gold in my cracks and He shined me. I looked better than I ever had, but my insides still needed to heal. That's why He kept me safe on the back shelf. I was His and only His from now on. No one would ever get a chance to use me again. He gave me such peace.

For most of my life, I felt as though no one could ever love me, just as the teapot was used, returned, used again, and thrown away. I would beg to be chosen, and in the end, each successive time, it felt as if I had no use or worth. I never felt good enough to be picked without my convincing them they should pick me.

Each person I dated or married misused me in a different way and then cast me aside. The potter faithfully picked me up and put me back together.

Arthur represented the last owner. When he was done with me, I was at my lowest. Given my life's disappointments and rejections, that was pretty low. I felt as though nothing could ever mend me. I was older now and my body was not as useful; it was rather weak and torn down.

Another part of putting me back together was the process of forgiving others who added to my brokenness.

My goal is to put others first. Whenever I trip and fall is when I put myself first or begin to worry about how I have messed up my life, or when I simply worry in general. My goal is to focus on the Lord and do whatever He asks me to say and do, so that when I face Him, He will say, "Well done." He's forgiven me so much, and I want to bring Him glory through my life rather than wasting any more time.

I am blessed by my birth daughter and God has given me three more daughters. He gave them all to me. He has kept me through the nightmare of an ex-wife and my belief that two people tried to kill me, including a husband. God has given me peace to forgive them all. Yes, I forgive them, for they do not know what they do.

One of the best and most difficult times of my life was the period of addressing those who needed to be forgiven and those I needed to ask for forgiveness. A few years after Arthur left, I went through the list of everyone in whose lives I caused an upheaval. I contacted everyone, either in person or by letter, whom I may have hurt in any way. And I asked for their forgiveness. Then I started getting calls from people who had hurt me and they were asking me to forgive them. It was a year of forgiving. It was a very exciting year! And yet, no, my two friends and ex, and his kids, nor his ex, never called. They will face God someday with it. I would not want to be in

Not in the fire

their shoes!

Next, I forgave debts that were owed to me, and it was an amazing experience. Men who had assaulted me at times when my housing arrangements made me particularly vulnerable contacted me and asked for my forgiveness. All were old and some were sick or dying and they wanted to apologize. One individual I had asked for forgiveness died two months after I contacted him. Sometimes, all I could say was that it wasn't them, that Satan orchestrated it all and they were just pawns in his horrible plans. Because God forgave me so much more, how could I not forgive so little in comparison?

I've learned to love my enemies the best I can and hope to keep on improving and perfecting that love. In Christ, all things are possible. I pray to see them as Christ sees them. Some represent more of a struggle than others, but my human forgiveness still leaves hurt. I still can feel ill when I see them. The pain they put me through still is palpable. I continue to be dependent on the Lord to heal.

God has given me new ministries that I love. He is faithful. He has given me four girls to care for, and I love watching them growing in their faith with God and becoming such lovely young ladies. I will talk about each one in the following chapters.

God Bless all who have purchased my book. The money will continue to help us. Thank you!

Chapter 32

<hr/>

Tonna Jean
My Peanut

Tonna was my joy, my only one for years. She was such a beautiful baby. I love her so much! I had so much fun with her, and she was all mine. I wanted her to have all I never had in life. I taught her about God from the beginning and through all of the good times and the difficult times as well. She went to Sunday school and Daily Vacation Bible school. She is loved and loving. She's had her own hard times, mostly with her health, but she felt losses as I did.

Tonna was pushed downstairs as a toddler at a friend's construction site. Our friend's little girl was so happy to see Tonna, she ran to her and Tonna lost her balance. Tonna tumbled and hit a nail that wasn't nailed securely. The nail is exactly where her head hit.

The wound was deep. At the hospital, they told us it had severed a nerve and the medical community didn't know when they could predict the full impact of the injury; perhaps it would be years. Years later, she was diagnosed with delayed reaction disorder. She would forever have to deal with this condition. Tonna is delayed in her perception of facts and situations. She loses her balance easily; she understands only part of every sentence, usually the first part. It is important to repeat whatever is said to her. She reacts slowly in every situation. She will never drive and no employer will hire her.

She once had a job with a friend in their restaurant in meal prep. Limited to four hours a shift, she did quite well. That restaurant closed and

Not in the fire

she has not been able to find work since. She has scoliosis, which has gotten worse over time, and she can't reach up or bend down. It is painful to pick up anything over ten pounds.

My old car had no seat belts and when she was five a drunk driver ran a red light, and I slammed on the brakes to avoid him. She went head first into the steering column and struck the right side of her head against the key. Since then, she has had petit mal seizures. There are medications that help the seizures, but they further slow her reaction time. She had trouble learning in school. The seizures ended by seventh grade, but she was so far behind they suggested that she apply to the regional technical school. She loved cooking and graduated at an eighth-grade level. No one informed us that she could be educated under state special education laws until age twenty-one. That information would have added years of education and could have helped her. I learned about the law many years down the road with her foster sister, Mary. Already mentioned was the incident with the moth balls, which she ate while my mother was watching her. My poor, sweet girl was assailed by life all around her, but she is gentle, is a prayer warrior, and has a full life with the help from her support dog. She has to live with me for the rest of her life. She will never have children and she so wanted to give me grandchildren. She is helpful at home, active in her church, and studies Hebrew. It is amazing that she can learn Hebrew. She has devoted friends from many places. I'm so proud of her.

Her dad called the year Arthur left in 1998. He wanted to talk to Tonna. She and I prayed about it and she decided she would talk to him. God is good. The contact led us to become friends again. Tonna met her three half-siblings and she told them all about her life in faith in Christ.

My cousin Diana, her kids, and my kids all went to Branson, MO, soon after we reestablished contact with Dwayne. We stopped in Fort Wayne and took Dwayne and his family out to dinner. When we left, we all hugged and cried. It was a poignant moment.

This is what I want to say to Tonna: Your sisters, Mary, Taylor and Rachel, are there for you. We may be a family of misfits, but we're here to take care of each other. We all love each other. We have had a lot of adventures in our life together. You have always been there for me and me for you. You are a big blessing. I love YOU, Tonna, so very much! Kisses and hugs. My peanut forever! Peanut, peanut butter, peanut, peanut, peanut, peanut butter our song! I'm the jelly that keeps us together.

I'm so immensely proud of you! God will be with you wherever you go.

And we'll have eternity in Heaven, no pain for either of us. Amen!

Love, Mom.

Not in the fire

Chapter 33

Mary
Shadow

Mary joined us first. Cindy and Joe, through the Department of Children and Families, asked me if I would take Mary and I agreed. She was so troubled that I needed an aide to assist her at school, on the bus, and to and from the bus. She had to sit near the driver.

Mary lived in a nightmare world before she came to live with me at ten years of age. There was no mention of how badly she had been abused until a few weeks after she arrived. Each new day added to my knowledge of how brutally she was treated.

Mary's mother was grossly obese and had limited mobility; she could not move or stand by herself. Most of her time was spent in the wheelchair and her boyfriend helped her. She hated Mary, and I don't know why anyone would hate Mary.

Mary was a beautiful little girl. The mom's boyfriend molested Mary at a young age. Not only did this mom fail to protect her daughter, but she also encouraged the abuse. Mary's brother also branded her with cigarette burns on her body.

At her mother's home, Mary was kept in a room by herself and fed finger foods exclusively. She had no idea how to use silverware. I had to teach her. She ate everything with her fingers at school and this was shocking to the other kids. They laughed at her and called her an animal, so she growled at them. She had been close to her dad before he died but was left to herself and the family weren't allowed to visit, so no one had any idea how bad her situation was.

When she lived at home she was made to kneel on rice or beans as a punishment. What offenses merited this kind of punishment is unknown. It caused growths on her knees and to this day she cannot kneel. We tried to have them removed, but the growths grew back.

Her mom put a bag on her head and told her she was ugly. This severely scarred her self-esteem. Her body was so encrusted with dirt that it took many attempts to clean through the crud. Her scalp appeared worse than any cradle cap one could imagine. I had to cut her hair because it was so matted. It had not been combed in a long time when she came to live with us.

Mary hated to bathe and though she was in foster care they were not allowed to make her bathe. I, on the other hand, had permission to do whatever I needed to help her. She was told in my presence that I was her last resort. If she did not let me help her, she was going to a lockdown just like her brother. Mary said she wanted to change and be normal.

Mary was so traumatized that she couldn't be around other children. She would attack others for looking at her. She barked and growled at them; it was her way of scaring them and making them stay away from her.

There were challenges that went beyond help getting to and participating in school. She engaged in other bizarre behaviors at home, as well. For instance, she stuffed as many rolls of toilet paper as she could fit in the toilet. I made her clean it out herself. She never did it again.

Mary has made strides towards growing up. She earned her high school diploma. She was graduated at a tenth-grade level. She had gotten far behind her age mates over the years so I let her graduate and didn't force her to stay where she was uncomfortable.

Mary took the driver's test twice and it took her four tries to pass the written test, however, it made no sense to grant her a license, but they did when the examiner said not to let her on the interstate and not to let her drive alone. As it turned out, she was scared. She would squeeze the steering wheel so tight she could hardly maneuver. She wouldn't go over fifteen miles an hour and the police kept stopping us and wondering how she got a license. One day she just told me, "I hate driving."

She once had a summer job, but only because her employers were friends. The next summer, my friend said she was sorry but Mary was so unpleasant to her customers she could not hire her back. Mary was nineteen years old then. For years, Mary has not wanted regular employment because of that experience. She is okay working for the church, which employs her to clean for a few hours a week. At the church she's alone and she can take

Not in the fire

her time. So it works. It has helped her self-esteem.

Finally, she can be in the presence of men she knows well and can tolerate a male seated beside her at times, but there is little hope she will function beyond the capacity of a mid-teen; she doesn't seem to mature in most areas of her life. When I say, "You really have to grow up," she answers, "How? I don't know how!" So, sadly, she is dependent on me. Thus, her nickname has always been Shadow.

Mary, at age 32, got a part-time job three days a week as a stocker at the gas station in town. I got the application, had her fill it out, and made her submit it to the gas station. She was hired next day. I went with her to the interview. She was scared but I encouraged her that she could succeed. She did for a time, but it was difficult. Her body suffered greatly, but the job helped her feel good about herself. It was encouraging, but it only lasted six months. Ultimately, she was fired because she sat down too often during her four-hour shift. So she was home with me again. During the writing of this memoir, she obtained a job working at a rest home where her uncle, my brother, is a resident. It is only a few hours a day, but we remain hopeful it will be good for her and her employer. Yet it's not looking good. She's so slow it takes her five-plus hours to do a one-hour shift. She has been cut down to four days a week and warned to move faster, or she'll need to decrease her hours again.

Mary, I am glad you're my daughter. I'm so sorry life was so cruel to you. I wish I had gotten you as a younger child. Remember, God is there to guide you, and Tonna is there for you, as are all of your sisters. Rachel and Taylor are there for you. I love you, Mary. You will and can do anything you put your hand to. Just don't give up! Keep trying to move faster. You have worked at Camp Pine Brooks ever since you were twenty years old; you move there, you can do it! Don't worry about getting married. You and Tonna can have each other's backs, sisters to the end! Trust God to help you.

Love, Mom.

Chapter 34

Taylor
Princess

My mom passed away from a heart attack at the age of 69. Vita, the little girl I had cared for while her father was in the service overseas, knew from Mom's obituary where Mom lived, and she knew I would be there. So, she got in touch with me the day of my mom's funeral. I agreed to meet her later in the week.

It was discouraging to see how totally messed up her life had become. Vita's grandmother, who had raised her, had also taken Vita's son away from her. At one time, Vita wanted to have me raise him, but the grandmother gave her money for him so that she could raise him. One wonders if they were concerned at all with what was best for him, but he is dead now. Though he did well for quite some time and even completed high school, he died of an overdose in his own bedroom. By that time, his grandmother had died and his mom and her husband lived with him.

Vita introduced me to her daughter, Taylor. Even with all I have seen over the years, the life Taylor was living, if it could be called a life, was horrendous to me. She wasn't fed when she cried, so she often crawled to the dog bowl and ate from that. She had sour milk bottles lying around that she tried to drink when she was hungry. She walked around naked with only caked-on filth covering her little body. Vita's excuse was that she couldn't afford diapers.

I asked, "Why don't you let me take her home for a few days while you get this place cleaned up?" I had to help in some way. "Oh, please. Thank

Not in the fire

you!" was her reply. Vita's friends told me to keep Taylor as long as I could for the kid's sake.

I washed Taylor first in a gas station bathroom before I brought her home. I bought her some clothes at the Salvation Army store and a few of the other items a toddler needs. I carried clothes and toys and a car seat in my car all the time, never knowing when I would get to take her with me again, which was soon after she returned home each time. I always took her to the gas station to bathe her. They became accustomed to seeing me there.

After this went on for a while, it became not a matter of days until I heard from Vita. It was often weeks that Taylor was with me, and then it was when I repeatedly called her. She finally responded and had me bring Taylor along with her to the welfare office. All she wanted was a welfare check, courtesy of Taylor.

Vita ended up in the hospital with a severe bout with asthma and had to be on a ventilator for a time. When she got out of the hospital she was afraid she would lose custody of Taylor. She didn't want a repeat performance from the grandmother, so Vita asked me if I would get joint custody of Taylor with her so if she died her grandmother wouldn't get her. I went to court when she was released from the hospital. Vita's intention was that if anything happened to her, I would get Taylor. What she didn't realize was that it also meant I would get Taylor if anything was wrong at Vita's home. She didn't get that part, but even though I could have abused the order, I didn't. I wanted to support her as a mother. I didn't know at the time it was going to be a lost cause. She had no idea how to improve her mothering skills.

At the time we reconnected, Taylor's father had been in jail. When he was released, they got engaged and I believe it was an attempt to take advantage of me. It wasn't just about money, they abused my friendship in so many ways. Not long after his release, they sent out announcements about their upcoming marriage… in my bed and breakfast. I only learned about it when I saw the announcement.

Running the bed and breakfast, along with cleaning jobs and private home health aide work, were how I put food on the table. When I broached the subject of the announcement, she added that they planned to move in with me, as well. She said I was the only mother she ever had and didn't think I would mind.

I said, "No you're not. I'll take care of Taylor. While you find a place to live, you can use my shed for storage, but that's the extent of it. You can't live here." I was firm about the move. "But you can have the wedding here." They lived in their car for a short time before they obtained a mobile home near me. I viewed the situation as tenuous, at best, but their move to the mobile home was when the situation went beyond anything I could have anticipated. They asked to have Taylor visit, so she went back and forth.

One day I picked her up, and Taylor herself was drunk. They'd left rum and Coke™ cups lying around from a recent party and Taylor drank them. They were high a lot of the time and I hated it. I confronted her husband, Hale, with how much I hated it. He had come to respect me because I tried to show him respect, which he had seldom experienced from anyone.

At one point, he and Vita had a terrible fight and he asked me to come and rescue Taylor. Meanwhile, Vita had called the police to put all of the blame on Hale.

When I arrived, I found out why they were fighting. Vita was pregnant. She claimed the baby was conceived after Hale got out of jail, which would mean Rachel would be born in June. She was born in May. Vita was the one screaming at him. Hale had a violent temper, and she knew how quickly he could become unstable. It was what caused him to be in and out of prison. He was a Level Three sex offender. He was adopted and also had been very abused by his birth parents.

Vita threatened that he would never see the kids, that she was sorry she married him. He picked up a knife and said, "You're the one who'll never see our kids again."

Once again, the Lord was with me as I did what I had to do. Without thinking, I jumped in front of him, put my hand up and grabbed his arm that held the knife to stop him. I said, "This isn't who you are. Now drop the knife. You're not going to go back to prison over this. You're better than that. You have a chance to prove you're better. Don't do this!"

Vita started yelling again. I turned to her and said, "Shut up. Just shut up. You've caused enough problems. Are you trying to get killed?" I believe with all of my heart that she was baiting him.

I said again, "Hale, this isn't who you are and you are scaring Taylor. Just drop the knife." Vita had a strong grip on her and would not let her go.

He dropped it and ran out the front door. Vita yelled after him, of course, "Well, the cops will pick you up on the road." She turned to me and said, "I called them before you got here."

"Really? And then you egged him on to the point of being violent?" She was trying to get him in jail.

The police indeed arrived. I gave a statement and told them what had happened. She had been pushing him verbally and physically. After the police left, Vita was out of control. She grabbed Taylor by the hand and was dragging her around. No matter how loud Taylor screamed, Vita wouldn't let me take her. I tried to take Taylor home.

I said, "Don't hurt her!" I was so worried about Taylor but had to leave her. "I'll leave now, but I'm picking her up in the morning. You take the time to calm down, clean up this mess and get yourself together. Don't let anything happen to that little girl, either."

The police found Hale and took him with them.

When I returned in the morning, Vita was on the phone to her therapist. She put me on the phone and I suggested a stay at the local hospital's behavioral health unit for her to get help; the therapist said that she agreed. I gathered them both in the car, helped Vita get admitted, and took Taylor home with me. By the time I left, Vita was refusing to talk to anyone.

On the way to the hospital, she had said she was sorry and that she was not in her right mind. She claimed she would be fine. I told her it would be in her best interest if she showed she was willing to work with them. After all, she called the therapist, not me. The therapist was obliged to call family services. Vita stayed for four weeks but still refused to cooperate in her care. So they released her. I refused to let Taylor go with her. Vita stayed in the mobile home until Hale was released. I got a nice letter from him while he was in jail. His parole officer was in touch with me on various occasions. I was in the middle of this nightmare. I had to do my best. I honestly believed he had a good side.

Ultimately, the mobile home park wouldn't let them live there any longer. They put their stuff into storage and lived on the streets or in a tent in the woods. So that Taylor would not have to live in a tent, I encouraged them to find an apartment. Taylor stayed with me and I took her for visits. Then they found a dumpy place that was part of a junkyard. There was only one bedroom so they couldn't have Taylor live with them. She visited, but she hated the visits and resorted to hitting herself to get her nose to bleed or screaming until they called me to come and get her. Finally, the Department of Children and Families filed a care and protection order on behalf of Taylor. Someone reported she was not being cared for when she was with them.

I was at the hearing and the judge graciously addressed me. I was frank with him. "They need drug and alcohol counseling. They need training on how to be parents. They need someone to teach them to clean their house at least enough to be safe for kids. And marriage counseling too."

So the judge turned to the assistant district attorney and said, "Make it happen."

I was astonished. Those two were put through their paces for the next five or six months. They complied and followed up for a time. When they were doing well, Taylor could visit. Once visitation was routine and firmly in place, they stopped doing the things they had been ordered to do. The irony is, they couldn't stand to have her for more than a few days, yet they tricked the system in order to get visitation.

Taylor hated being with them and once again resorted to self-harm to protest. One time she crammed her fingers up her nose to create a nose bleed. Other times she hammered herself in the face and banged her head against the wall. Any of those incidents was all it would take for them to call me. Taylor knew producing blood would freak them out and they became afraid of being charged with abuse again. It reached the point where I told them that Taylor could visit for only short periods of time with them, and I would stay with her to supervise.

When the baby arrived, they insisted that Taylor, Hale's mom, grandmother, and I be present. So we all went and were present for Rachel's birth. Vita showed no emotion; she didn't seem to be happy in the least. Taylor had the privilege of naming the baby and she named her after her best friend at the time. She and I left without holding Rachel or even getting close to her. There would be all new ways they would use me and I didn't want to get too attached to the baby.

Even after Vita and Rachel were home, I was determined to keep my distance. I was sure they would manipulate me to care for her and subsequently deprive me of contact with her. I wasn't sure a baby could survive in their current lifestyle. I was so torn and I decided to leave Rachel in God's hands.

Soon, Hale called and told me Rachel wouldn't eat, that she was sick all of the time and that she screamed all night. I told him to take her to the doctor. The doctor called me at their request saying I was Vita's mother. I told him that wasn't true, but I was an old foster mother. He told me if Rachel didn't eat soon, she would die. He said she was failing to thrive. I made sure he knew they were the ones who needed to hear that. I was sad and I gave it over to God.

I was at the wedding of our pastor's daughter when Hale walked into the reception and handed me a two-week old baby. He said, "You have to take her, too, or she will die." Then he walked out. No baby supplies, no food, nothing. She was down to four and a half pounds.

Pastor sent me home with some supplies from the church nursery and other folks donated items we needed. I signed up for Women, Infants and Children assistance (WIC) for both girls. The Department of Children and Families had me bring Rachel for visits to Vita and Hale, but no overnights. At a visit when she was one-month old, she screamed, and Hale shook her to "shut her up." A neighbor called police and DCFS called me to come back and get her. They went to court again. He was charged with shaking Rachel and once again of neglect of Taylor. The judge said no more visits for Taylor unless I felt it was safe and none at all for Rachel. I was given full custody of both girls.

Then they nearly burned down their apartment. They were charging homeless people to use the dryer until it over-heated. Needless to say, they got kicked out. Then they found another small house to live in after four months of hotels and five months of living in a camper.

Once they were in the new house, DCFS called us all into court and told the judge that they were taking the kids for adoption. The agency thought they had done all they could and for the safety of the kids, they determined these two could not be parents. The judge by now was familiar with me and asked if I wanted the kids. I said yes, and it was so ordered.

Full custody and no visits. The court asked if I would need help. I was about to say yes, but Hale's mother, who showed up for the hearing, told the court she would help me. She stated that she was well-off and that money wasn't a problem. So I got custody and she never helped me after a few times. Her interest died off fast. God has helped me, as well as friends and my church. We pulled together.

After infuriating a host of people, Vita and Hale disappeared, owing rent and many other debts, of course. They lost so much over the years. Things could have been so different if they'd only wanted to change. I brought them to church a few times. It really saddens me, but I love these girls and they are mine now. I told Vita that the only thing I could do for her was to raise her girls.

This is a very brief description of my years with them in my life. The last eleven years we haven't heard from their parents. I did a lot for them besides caring for the girls. From getting them food, money, doing laundry, taking them to doctors and knee surgery for Hale, I went above and beyond for them, but it didn't change them.

Taylor used to call me "Gammie" for the first five years. When Rachel was born, she wanted to call me "Momma." I said I'd be honored. Rachel has only known me as a mom.

Taylor has had learning problems but has worked hard and persisted in her education. Memories of trauma, coupled with her struggles with learning issues, have made life difficult for her at times, but God has helped her to grow and overcome many of her battles.

Taylor graduated in 2020 but the COVID-19 pandemic hit the world and caused her to lose her graduation celebrations. She met Dylan about seven years ago. He is a nice young man who has progressed from a friend to more than a friend. They plan on getting married and living with me in the meanwhile. Their wedding day is June 25, 2022 and I look forward to it. His family are all such nice people. I now have a son-in-law! Taylor has her driver's license and is working at a nearby adventure area. Her discount provides our family with a variety of activities from whitewater rafting to an array of ziplines.

Young lady, I am so proud of how you have turned so many bad things into great things; you will excel in anything you put your heart to. Go Girl! I love you so much! My princess! I love you!

Love, Mom/Gammie.

Not in the fire

Chapter 35

Rachel

Sunshine/Button/Little Biscuits/Storm Cloud/Tiger! She wears many hats this one! The joy of my old age.

Vita and Hale stayed out of my life in the months leading up to the new baby. I knew drugs were part of the scene, and I simply trusted God to take care of His little one. Their choices were far out there, all bad to me, it seemed. They didn't see it that way but they knew I did.

As I said, I was sure this little baby could never make it under the circumstances, and that's why I was reluctant to bond with her. Within a week, the doctor informed Vita that Rachel was failing to thrive. The doctor who treated Rachel also treated Taylor and he told me that this baby would die if they couldn't figure out how to get her to eat..

There was no way Vita would get up to feed a baby in the middle of the night or even in the morning. Both parents slept until at least lunchtime--the impact of booze and drugs. A baby did not fit their lifestyle. Any attempts at feeding prompted Rachel to upchuck. I presumed many things were responsible, including milk tainted with drugs or bacteria. She tried to breastfeed, even after being told not to because of the medications she was prescribed.

Rachel weighed seven pounds when she was born. Within a week, she weighed only six pounds and lost another pound the following week. The doctor made it clear that they had to feed her regularly. As mentioned earlier,

Hale brought her to me at Pastor Chuck's daughter's wedding and said, "You have to take her or she's going to die." He then handed her to me and left.

Once Rachel was with me, and with around-the-clock feedings and constant holding, Rachel began eating. After the shaking incident with Hale, I sensed something was wrong. She was not responsive and she didn't focus on me or objects around her. She simply stared.

I took her to the doctor immediately and they said she had Shaken Baby Syndrome, causing blindness. They seemed to think, given time, she would see again.

It was a relief that I no longer had to take the girls for visits but Rachel wasn't out of the woods. She was fearful and cried every waking moment unless I held her. I swaddled her close to me as I went about my life. Everywhere I went,-even at church and in choir, she was in my front carrier. After a few weeks, she could remain calm for short periods with Mary or Tonna holding her. She still screamed when placed in car seat. The doctor said she needed to be close to me because she couldn't see. The doctors were confident she would see again, and it was such an answer to prayer when her sight returned at six months of age. It was one of the most joyful times to see her look at me and smile when I took a photo. I looked at her and said, "You can see me, can't you?" She just followed me all around the room. She has not ceased being my happy child since then.

She also began to thrive and learn to be content, even if not in my arms on a constant basis. What a joy it is to see she is still happy now as a joyful and healthy teenager; she truly is thriving.

I tried to remain part of Vita's and Hale's lives. I wanted to help if I could. I took them to doctor's appointments and encouraged them to attend church, but whenever they came close to the car, Taylor dropped to the floor out of sight. Eventually they disappeared from our lives. They were in too deep with debts and they had lots of people upset with them. They owed money and eventually had to get out of town. In the meantime, they used the girls' social security numbers in order to set up new accounts. I was familiar with this scam. My mother had done the same thing. When I started getting the bills based on their use of the kids' social security numbers and our address, in defense of the kids' reputations, I filed charges against them.

Hale's mother has kept in touch and I call her, as well. At least she remembers birthdays and Christmas. She told me, not surprisingly, Vita's son, Troy, from her first marriage died of a drug overdose. Her Troy was dead. Taylor remembered him and was sad. Taylor, however, was frightened at the thought of seeing her parents, and Rachel doesn't know who they are. So we did not try to go to Troy's funeral. Nor did we want to see Vita's father, Robert, who did not care for his own daughter. He died a few years later of cancer. He had been addicted to drugs and drunk for much of his life. He had tried to do rehab so many times over the years.

He sent me a letter telling me he was sorry for the way he acted years ago when he hurt me. He still wished I had kept Vita. He also spent time in jail for various crimes. I felt sad for him. He used to be fun and caring. He now was bitter and angry. I told him to go to a church, which he did. The folks at church took him in and cared for him for a short time until he died. I was grateful I had his two granddaughters, and I planned a good future for them.

At least he found God. Amen! I still had fond memories of when he was a ham radio operator and he got me into it as well. He would have gotten a kick out of the fact that Rachel also is a ham radio operator. She is in a junior weathercaster's club, as well. He loved music and played in a hard rock band. Rachel plays five instruments and Taylor plays two. Someday in heaven he'll see his grandchildren and we all will praise God together. Amen!

Rachel is a Girl Scout, as was Taylor, who has been in scouts for twelve years; she bridged to adult. Rachel will bridge in fall 2022 and has two years to go. Rachel loves to earn awards and sell Girl Scout cookies. She's been the top seller in her troop for six years. She raised enough money to provide fifty Leap Pads and stuffed animals for kids with cancer in Boston hospitals for her bronze award. She also raised money for the Covenant House Shelter in New York City and participated by planting flowers in a "save the bees" project for her silver award. She obtained donations from businesses for the Veterans Mall in Greenfield, MA., and she received an award for an essay contest on her ideas on our government. Most were impressed but some were upset because she wrote in support of former President Trump's policies. She was awarded a check in a ceremony with the vets. She is working on bullying and racial issues in school for her gold award, the top award given in Girl Scouts.

Plus, Rachel plans to go to college. She loves soccer, tennis and volleyball. She can play four instruments but COVID ended all that. Someday, she'll pick it up again.

She is going to have a great life. She wants to be a golf pro, a music teacher, and a veterinarian who has free clinics for people who can't afford a veterinarian. She also is doing web design. She wants to major in web design and minor in veterinary medicine in college. She also got a work permit at 16 to work at a vet clinic. She has big plans, and it will be fun seeing what she does.

Her teachers love her. I got a letter from her principal stating how proud they were of her accomplishments and that she was a joy. She is working on weekends at a nearby ski/adventure area and she hopes to earn enough to pay for a trip to Italy this summer with the Girls Scouts.

You go for the gold my sweet girl! I love you so very much. Don't ever forget to pass on to your kids all our kisses you invented, bubble kiss, woohoo kiss, butterfly kiss, giggle kiss, Eskimo kiss. Remember my favorites, belly, belly, belly, piggy, piggy, piggy spider on the head, and ant in the ear (She's the only kid to ever have to go to the doctor to get an ant taken out of her ear!) and biscuits, biscuits, biscuits. You have made life so fun; keep it up. Love you a bushel and a peck and a hug around the neck and woodless and oodles of noodles! Ha! Gotcha!

Love you soooo much, Mom.

Epilogue

IN CONCLUSION I WANT TO LEAVE YOU WITH THIS:

As you read this story about part of my life, you will see that the choices I made were not always good for me or those around me. Those choices molded me into who I am. Readers, your choices will also help to make you who you are. Be sure to add the most important ingredient -- God! He came into my life early on and many more bad things would have happened if not. Yes, unfortunate things still happen. That's life. Because of God in my life, the way I viewed the problems was also different. I never held onto hostility, anger, or bitterness. Though I often questioned the choices of others, resentment would have had me in therapy for my whole life. So, make good choices for you and your loved ones. Above all else, please, find God.

Who pays the price?

Before we are born, we already begin to suffer the choices of the parent that carries us by how they take care of their body and manage their lives.

When we are born, the cycle starts of life-long payments, whether for diapers or other baby needs, doctor bills, hospital bills, and food, just to name a few of the expenses. As individuals grow, the bills grow throughout all of childhood.

Adulthood and independence require the individual to cover their own expenses: schooling, housing, heat, food, energy, transportation, insurance, clothing, medical expenses, taxes. Nothing is free.

It costs to dispose of waste at the sewer department, transfer station, and garbage dump; all of the old, useless items in our lives cost to be disposed of. Just let's not dispose of our children. That fetus could have been a great person who fixed things in and around this world. We don't know that. It's better to give the life of a child to so many that can't have children and watch and see the things that child will do. Killing it should never me an option, in my mind.

Some can afford the luxuries of life and others can't afford the same luxuries. Often it seems that the latter are happier inside. Perhaps they have found what others are still trying to buy with money. It is the poor who often are the first to give the shirt off their backs for those in need. They live for today. The rich take care for their riches, yet tomorrow may never come for them, and someone else may enjoy their wealth.

Elder-care costs are another layer, and those who care for the elderly often make the choices. Then there will be a funeral, burial, and provisions to care for the upkeep on the burial plots. Oh that there is enough left to leave the next generation of loved ones a nest egg, but they will determine their own paths.

We've hopefully spent our lives training them better to survive and care for each other. Then the cycle starts all over in their life of paying.

Here is the biggest price: Where will an individual spend all of eternity? Did they find Christ before death?

For those who have not found Christ, sadly it is then too late. Then there is only endless consuming fires with individuals begging for a drop of water to quench their thirst. Better described, it is eternal separation from God for refusing God's gift --His Son, Jesus. He came and died for all. He PAID the price so we could be free from the debt we owe. His gift gives those who know Him eternal separation from sin and hell.

Why spend eternity in hell when eternity in His glorious heaven --a new earth-- is being prepared. WOW! Why would anyone choose separation? The only explanation is that they are deceived into believing in many other lies about ways to heaven. But the end of that journey is not heaven, it is HELL! It is plain and simple because GOD says His son is the only way. There is no other. So please wake up and face the facts before it's too late. Please, for those of you who want to believe, say this prayer:

Dear Father in Heaven,

Please forgive me of my sins and bad choices in this life you gave me. Please come into my heart and live with me. Help me to change my life. I want to be with you in heaven.

Amen!

Remember, you won't change overnight, though some have. But most change a small amount at a time because they have so much to work on. God doesn't expect us to deal with it all at once. Listen to the "still, small voice;" you need to be quiet to hear Him. And test what you hear. If it's not in His Word, The Bible, do not listen, it's a lie from Satan to pull you away. But remember God says He will never let us be pulled out of His hands. Simply claim that promise. Also, if you sing *Jesus Loves Me* --everyone knows that one, or any hymn-- Satan will flee. He hates music that praises God. He also hates prayer. So pray. Talk to God all day long. Ask Him for help in all things. Believe me, He cares and He will answer. Also find a good church that preaches God's word. There are many churches that do not. So be careful. Good luck, and I'll see you in heaven. Welcome to the family of GOD. AMEN!

For those of you who still don't believe, I'm heartbroken for you. I pray before you die you will change your mind, and even at your last breath, as you see hell before you and fear fills your soul, accept Him then. If it's genuine, God will accept you. He'll know if your faith is real. Just say, "Please God, accept me. I ask for forgiveness." I pray you do and mean it. It's not done out of fear only.

God be with you and may He keep trying to reach you in life. AMEN!

Last but not least, I want to share a poem my mother wrote for me before she died. I had it published and it won an award.

In memory of Florence Marie Grover

I had great respect and admiration for all her talents in life that she sadly never got to use. But thank you for trying the best you could; you suffered a lot in life. You chose to follow Christ, and that was the best choice you ever made. I will see you in Heaven MOM. Say 'hi' to Dad and everyone who is there with you.

To my Daughter, Barbara Jean Austin:

Once I was a mother, a mother dear was I

Till fate began to use me, only name did I belie.

I gave birth to a baby, six darlings did I conceive,

Though two were taken from me, two others came to be.

I nursed and pampered all of them, how stubborn they could be,

But everyone among us, knew the mother was me.

Times that came, times that went, much happiness was often spent.

But soon after graduation, the wedding bells for bride and gent.

But now I seem so lonely, for I made the child my life.

I've never had the loving care or been important as a wife!

So now I sit and wonder and I wonder why I sit?

The kids are gone forever, and mother doesn't fit.

If only dreams were good enough to fill these empty hours,

Or I was just remembered, and it was really in my power.

Although I don't regret it, it's a wish I have learned.

To be the mother once again, is all that I'm concerned.

About Kharis Publishing:

Kharis Publishing, an imprint of Kharis Media LLC, is a leading Christian and inspirational book publisher based in Aurora, Chicago metropolitan area, Illinois. Kharis' dual mission is to give voice to under-represented writers (including women and first-time authors) and equip orphans in developing countries with literacy tools. That is why, for each book sold, the publisher channels some of the proceeds into providing books and computers for orphanages in developing countries so that these kids may learn to read, dream, and grow. For a limited time, Kharis Publishing is accepting unsolicitedqueries for nonfiction (Christian, self-help, memoirs, business, health and wellness) from qualified leaders, professionals, pastors, and ministers. Learnmore at: About Us - Kharis Publishing - Accepting Manuscript

www.ingramcontent.com/pod-product-compliance
Lightning Source LLC
Chambersburg PA
CBHW062105080426
42734CB00012B/2760